£9·95

PIAGET'S THEORY OF COGNITIVE AND AFFECTIVE DEVELOPMENT

PIAGET'S THEORY OF COGNITIVE AND AFFECTIVE DEVELOPMENT

THIRD EDITION

BARRY J. WADSWORTH

MOUNT HOLYOKE COLLEGE

With Drawings by the Author

Longman
New York & London

Piaget's Theory of Cognitive and Affective Development
Third Edition

Longman Inc., 1560 Broadway, New York, N.Y. 10036
Associated companies, branches, and representatives
throughout the world.

Developmental Editor: Nicole Benevento
Editorial and Design Supervisor: James Fields
Production/Manufacturing: Ferne Y. Kawahara

Library of Congress Cataloging in Publication Data

Wadsworth, Barry J.
    Piaget's theory of cognitive and affective development.

    Rev. ed. of: Piaget's theory of cognitive development. 2nd
ed. c1979.
    Bibliography: p.
    Includes index.
    1. Cognition in children.   2. Emotion in children.
3. Piaget, Jean, 1896–1980.   I. Wadsworth, Barry J.
Piaget's theory of cognitive development. II. Title.
BF723.C5W33 1984   155.4'13'0924   83-13637
ISBN 0-582-28425-2

Manufactured in the United States of America
Printing: 9 8 7 6 5 4 3 2 1
Year: 91 90 89 88 87 86 85 84 83

To Jean Piaget and Stephen Davol—
Two men who understood children, development,
and how to help others learn

CONTENTS

PREFACE

This book has evolved out of the first two editions of *Piaget's Theory of Cognitive Development* (New York: Longman, 1971, 1979). Its aim remains the same as that of the two earlier editions: to introduce the education or psychology student to Jean Piaget's theory in an undistorted, conceptual manner. However, while the earlier books focused primarily on Piaget's work on cognitive or intellectual development, this volume also examines Piaget's extensive studies on affective development, a rich body of work that has largely been overlooked by psychologists and educators. I have also incorporated the most important developments in Piagetian theory of the last ten years. My goal is to show the reader that there are many rewards in understanding Piaget's work.

Piaget painted a compelling picture of how children construct and acquire knowledge. This conception was based on sixty years of rigorous observation, thought, and research by one of the most creative and insightful minds of this century. Scientists generally agree that Piaget pushed the frontiers of psychological thought as far as any one person ever has. Educators and child psychologists agree that he has led us to an important new understanding of children's development. Regardless of their professional position, those who work with children (and adults) have the potential to be more effective if they understand how and why children behave as they do. Piaget and his advocates have contributed much to that understanding.

As an elementary school teacher initially, I had doubts about some of the educational practices I engaged in. My intuitions frequently took a direction that my peers and tradition did not want to follow. Because of my discovery of Piaget's work, I have developed a better understanding of children, the educational process, and where my intuitions properly fit. My hope is that this book will similarly assist you.

I began to write about Piaget's work in 1969 as a college teacher who believed it was important for education and psychology students to become familiar with Piaget's ideas. Now, as then, several people were instrumental in helping me with this book. I am indebted to Sukey Heard and Marilyn Gass at Mount Holyoke College for their careful reading of the manuscript and for their suggestions. I wish to thank Arthur Nicholson for his willingness to talk and make suggestions. This writing would not have been accomplished without the support of Mount Holyoke College during a sabbatical year. Particular credit is given Eva Wadsworth, who has continuously provided sound criticism and advice and support for my work. Finally, I appreciate the help I have received from Nicole Benevento and Irene Glynn at Longman.

Barry J. Wadsworth

PIAGET'S THEORY OF COGNITIVE AND AFFECTIVE DEVELOPMENT

INTRODUCTION

Jean Piaget's college and university training was in the natural sciences. His main interests originally were in biology. Early in his career he became interested in children's intellectual development, and he spent the last sixty years of his life gathering an impressive amount of research information pertaining to mental development. His work produced an elaborate and comprehensive theory of how intelligence develops.[1]

In America, Piaget is thought of primarily as a child psychologist and educator. In the strict sense, he was neither. His work was not directly concerned with predicting behavior, as the psychologist's frequently is, nor was he directly concerned with how to teach children. He preferred to be classified as a genetic epistemologist.[2] His work was primarily concerned with describing and explaining in a very systematic way the growth and development of intellectual structures and knowledge. It is not surprising that his work has had a great impact on education and psychology, both here and abroad.

Piaget's publications, all written originally in French, took many years to cross the Atlantic. Only since the 1960s have Piaget's works and Piagetian concepts spread quickly throughout American educational and psychological thought. L'Abate's 1968 frequency of citation study[3] is a

1

measure of the impact of Piaget's works on American thought. L'Abate's search of journals and textbooks in the child development field during the 1950s and 1960s found Piaget to be the most frequently cited author. A more recent study, undertaken in 1979 by the author of this book and similar to L'Abate's, also found Piaget to be the most frequently cited author.

BIOGRAPHY

Piaget's life was one of scholarship and hard work. He was born in 1896 in Neuchatel, Switzerland. By his own admission, he was an intellectually precocious youth. At age 10 he managed his first publication, a description of a partly albino sparrow he observed in a public park. To some extent, the direction and rigor of Piaget's efforts were determined early in his life. At age 15, he decided to direct his work toward a biological explanation of knowledge, a goal that is clearly reflected in his work.

In 1915, at age 18, Piaget received his baccalaureate from the University of Neuchatel. Three years later, he received a doctorate in the natural sciences from the same school. Much of his study was in philosophy. During this period, Piaget studied the development of mollusks in the many lakes around Neuchatel. He was interested in how mollusks adapted to being transferred from one environment to another. He discovered that their shell structure was affected by rough or calm lake water; the shell structure changed as the environment changed. By age 21, he had published twenty-five professional papers (mostly on mollusks) and was considered one of the world's few experts on mollusks.

His intensive work in biology led him to conclude that biological development was due not only to maturation (and heredity) but also to variables in the environment. He observed in successive generations of mollusks certain structural changes that could only be attributed to movement from large lakes with much wave action to small ponds with little or no wave action. Such observations convinced

Piaget that biological development was a process of adaptation to the environment; it could not be explained by maturation alone (Piaget 1952b, p. 250). These experiences and convictions contributed to Piaget's later view of mental development as primarily a process of adaptation to the environment and an extension of biological development.[4]

Soon after completing his doctorate, Piaget turned to psychology. He had become convinced that there were severe limits to philosophy. He was most concerned that philosophical solutions to problems could not be verified without experimental work. For several years he had been reading and taking classes in psychology, and he had become increasingly interested in the field. He went to Zurich in 1918, where he studied and worked in psychological clinics, immersing himself in psychological experimentation. In 1919 he went to Paris and spent two years at the Sorbonne. While in Paris, he had a chance to work in Binet's[5] laboratory (a grade school), standardizing several tests. Unenthusiastic at first, he became intrigued with the incorrect answers children gave to questions on the tests; shortly thereafter, he was hard at work examining the reasoning processes underlying children's responses.

Piaget had found his research interest; he was convinced that the development of children's intelligence could be studied experimentally. For two years he continued testing children, examining the development of their thought.

> At last I had found my field of research. First of all it became clear to me that the theory of the relations between the whole and the part can be studied experimentally through the analysis of the psychological processes underlying logical operations [logical reasoning]. This marked the end of my "theoretical" period and the start of an inductive and experimental era in the psychological domain which I had always wanted to enter, but for which until then I had not found the suitable problems. (Ibid., p. 245)

In 1921 Piaget was offered the directorship of studies at the Institut J. J. Rousseau in Geneva, a position that proved to be the perfect environment for his studies. He was launched on a course of research that did not change: the investigation of the mental development of children. Piaget's research and writing on this issue filled most of his professional work for the next sixty years.

By the time he was thirty, Piaget was famous for his works in psychology.[6] Through the years he conducted continuous research and taught at the University of Geneva. A prolific writer, he published many books and hundreds of journal articles, several in conjunction with the colleagues he assembled in Geneva. He attributed much of his productivity to those who worked with him over the years.

Piaget was an untiring worker. Until his death in 1980 he followed a strenuous, self-imposed work schedule. Each summer, when the school year ended, he collected his research findings for the year and headed for an abandoned farmhouse in the Alps where he spent the summer in isolation, writing and walking, his whereabouts unknown but to a few friends and his family. When the summer ended, he returned from the mountains with a new book or two plus several articles (Elkind 1968).

Piaget was honored around the world. He received honorary degrees from Harvard (1936), the Sorbonne (1946), the University of Brussels (1949), Brazil (1949), and from Columbia (1970). In 1969 he was the first European cited by the American Psychological Association; the citation was for his distinguished contribution to psychology. Before his death, he made several trips to the United States to address American groups concerned with child development.

In 1955, with the help of a grant from the Rockefeller Foundation, the International Center for Genetic Epistemology was established in Geneva. Each year this program permits a number of eminent scholars to visit and do research with the Geneva group that grew up around Piaget; several Americans have studied under the program. Piaget always insisted that knowledge was best pursued from an interdisciplinary perspective. Thus the scholars working at the Center are specialists in several fields: physics, biology, mathematics, and language, as well as psychology and education.

Whether time proves Piaget's basic assumptions to be correct or incorrect, his works have generated more interest and research than those of any other person in psychology in the last sixty years.

Jean Piaget died in Geneva on September 16, 1980. He was eighty-four years old.

THE APPROACH TO RESEARCH

Piaget was a developmental psychologist in that he was concerned with uncovering the ontogenetic[7] changes in cognitive functioning from birth through adolescence. His works were slow to gain wide attention in the United States. Aside from the fact that they were written in French, the reasons for this are largely related to the nature of his theory and research methodology. The concepts he used did not gain acceptance easily in America; neither did his "experimental" methodology.

Psychology in the United States has had a strong tradition of behaviorism. Men such as Thorndike, Tolman, Watson, Hull, Spence, and Skinner have dominated the scene, each primarily interested in stimulus-response relationships and the concept of reinforcement. Traditionally, American psychologists of the behaviorist school have not inferred the existence of internal mental processes (of thought).

Such Piagetian concepts as assimilation were entirely foreign to the behaviorist position. Piaget did not conceptualize behavior in terms of stimuli and responses, and he did not use the construct of reinforcement. Some important Piagetian concepts (to be explained in the next chapter) are schemata, assimilation, accommodation, and equilibration. Also, Piaget did infer the existence of internal mental processes. It was difficult for many American psychologists to come to grips with such concepts.

In America, experimental research in psychology typically concerned itself with hypothesis testing, rigorous control of experimental variables, and treatment of data with sophisticated statistical procedures. Most of Piaget's research was not experimental in these ways. He did not typically employ elaborate statistics to test hypotheses nor use control groups in his research. From his work in Paris in Binet's clinic, Piaget evolved a clinical-descriptive technique that became a trademark for his work. It essentially involved asking individual children carefully selected questions and noting their responses. In other cases, data were nothing more than the observation of infant behavior. It was difficult for American psychologists to consider these techniques experimental because Piaget's methodology bore little resemblance to American experimental psychology. Piaget's work was basically observational, though it was invariably systematic and his analyses were exceedingly detailed; they were designed to detect developmental changes in cognitive functioning.

Especially in his early work, Piaget frequently permitted himself to be led by his "intuition" when interviewing children. In the clinical approach, any two children are not necessarily asked the same questions in the same setting. In effect, no two children ever receive the same experimental treatment. *The Child's Conception of the World* (1929) is an example of Piaget's skillful selection of questions. The book is without statistical tables, and "sample sizes" are small. The main sources for two of Piaget's books[8] were observations of his own three children, who were born between 1925 and 1931. These meticulous observations provided him with an awareness of the relationship between early sensori-motor actions and later cognitive development. From these exceedingly complete and careful descriptions of behavior over a period of years, he drew major conclusions regarding intellectual development from birth to age 2. This type of research was severely criticized because of the small sample size, and because it was not considered experimental. The criticisms diminish in importance if one accepts the assumption implicit in Piaget's theory: that the general course of development of intellectual structures is the same in all persons. If this is true, then sample sizes become meaningless.[9] There is considerable merit in using the longitudinal approach that Piaget used. Although he frequently observed small numbers of children, his observations of the same subjects on occasion ranged over years.

While much of Piaget's early work can be looked upon as intuitive, employing nonexperimental procedures and using small samples of subjects, a large part of his later work was as rigorously experimental as any psychologist might wish. *The Early Growth of Logic in the Child* (1964) and *The Mechanisms of Perception* (1969) carefully report statistical findings and respectable sample sizes. The material reported in *The Growth of Logical Thinking from Childhood to Adolescence* (1958) is based on the testing of over 1500 subjects.

Many criticisms have been leveled at Piaget's approach to research, but no one has disputed that it is systematic, rigorous, and insightful. Piaget's primary technique was one of systematic observation, description, and analysis of children's behavior. This approach is primarily designed to discover the nature and level of development of the concepts children use, not to produce developmental scales. Piaget defended his approach to research on the basis that it is the most appropriate for the questions he wished to answer. This sounds very reasonable, but it does not always rest well with those who believe American experimental procedures are the "only" correct ones.

THE ORGANIZATION OF THE BOOK

One of the difficulties encountered by the uninitiated in reading Piaget's works is the number of unique concepts he used to conceptualize behavior. It is necessary to understand these concepts before his works can be understood. Chapter 1 describes four concepts that are central to all Piaget's work: schema, assimilation, accommodation, and equilibration. Chapter 2 deals with the relationship betweeen cognitive development and factors such as heredity, action, motivation, and stages of development.

Chapters 3 through 6 each deal with one of the four stages of cognitive and affective development in the order in which they occur. Chapter 7 discusses the relationship of cognitive and affective development to adolescent behavior. Chapter 8 summarizes the previous chapters and discusses some of the implications of Piaget's works for child training and education.

NOTES

1. In this book the terms *intellectual, cognitive,* and *mental* are used interchangeably.

2. Genetic epistemology is the science of how knowledge is acquired.

3. Two journals, *Child Development* (1950–65) and *Journal of Genetic Psychology* (1957–58, 1960–65), were searched, along with twelve popular and current textbooks on child development.

4. Mental development as a form of adaptation in the biological sense, one of Piaget's revolutionary and most important concepts, is discussed in Chapter 2.

5. Binet is considered the father of the Binet Intelligence Test from which current forms of the Stanford-Binet were derived.

6. *The Language and Thought of the Child* and *Judgment and Reasoning of the Child* (both 1924) were Piaget's first books on psychology, though earlier he had published numerous papers in the field.

7. *Ontogenetic*: developmental changes that occur in the individual.

8. *Play, Dreams, and Imitation in Childhood* (1951) and *The Origins of Intelligence in Children* (1952).

9. Considerable evidence exists that the *course* of cognitive development is basically the same in *all* people, with some variation reflective of culture (see Dasen 1977 for a review of research on this topic).

Chapter 1

INTELLECTUAL ORGANIZATION AND ADAPTATION

Piaget's system for conceptualizing cognitive development was greatly influenced by his early training and work as a biologist. Functioning as a biologist, he became vividly aware of, and impressed by, the interaction of mollusks with their environment. Mollusks, like all living organisms, constantly adapt to changes in environmental conditions.

From this early work, Piaget came to believe that biological acts are acts of *adaptation* to the physical environment and *organizations* of the environment. He also came to believe that the mind and body do not operate independently of one another and that mental activity is subject to the same laws that, in general, biological activity is. This led him to conceptualize intellectual development in much the same way as biological development. He saw cognitive acts as acts of *organization* of and *adaptation* to the environment. This does not imply in any sense that mental behavior can be attributed completely to biological functioning, but that the concepts of biological development are useful and valid for looking at intellectual development. Indeed, Piaget asserted that the basic principles of cognitive development are the *same as those of biological development*. Organization and adaptation were not viewed by Piaget as separate processes.

> From the biological point of view organization is inseparable from adaptation: They are two complementary processes of a single mechanism, the first being the internal aspect of the cycle of which adaptation constitutes the external aspect. (Piaget 1952c, p. 7)

For Piaget, intellectual activity could not be separated from the "total" functioning of the organism. Thus, he considered intellectual functioning to be a special form of biological activity (ibid., p. 42). Intellectual and biological activity are both part of the overall process by which an organism adapts to the environment and organizes experience.

To begin to understand the processes of intellectual organization and adaptation as they were viewed by Piaget, four basic concepts must be grasped. They are the concepts of *schema*, *assimilation*, *accommodation*, and *equilibration*. These concepts are used to explain how and why mental development occurs.

SCHEMA

Piaget believed that the mind has structures much in the same way that the body does. All animals have a stomach, a structure that permits eating and digestion. To help explain why children (all persons) make rather stable responses to stimuli, and to account for many of the phenomena associated with memory, Piaget used the word *schema*. Schemata (the plural of schema) are the cognitive or mental *structures* by which individuals intellectually adapt to and organize the environment. As structures, *schemata* are the mental counterparts of biological means of adapting. The stomach is a biological structure that animals use successfully to adapt to their environment. In much the same way, schemata are structures that adapt and change with mental development. These structures are inferred to exist. They are constructs in the same way that Freud's Id and Ego are.[1]

Schemata can be simplistically thought of as concepts or categories. Another analogy might be an index file in which each index card represents a schema. Adults have many cards or schemata. These schemata are used to process and identify incoming stimuli. In this way the organism is able to differentiate between stimulus events and to generalize. When a child is born, it has few schemata (cards on file). As the child develops, his or her schemata gradually become more generalized, more differentiated, and progressively more "adult."

Schemata never stop changing or becoming more refined. Indeed, the sensori-motor schemata of childhood develop into the schemata of adulthood. Picture, if you will, an index file in a child's head. At birth it contains only a few large cards on which everything is written. As the child develops, more cards are necessary to contain the changing classifications. As an illustration, imagine a child walking down a country road with his father. The father looks into a field nearby and sees what adults call a cow. He says to his son, "John, look at that animal. What is it?" John looks into the field and sees the cow. One can almost see the wheels going around in the child's head when he is thinking. After a moment of thought, John says, "It's a dog." Assuming John made an honest response, we could infer something like this: John looked out into the field and saw a cow. Presented with this "new" stimulus (he had never seen a cow before), he tried to place the stimulus in reference to a card in his card file. In terms of the things John could identify, the stimulus (cow) most closely approximated a dog, so he identified the object as a dog (a schema or file).

In Piaget's terms we would say that the child has a number of schemata. These schemata are analogous to concepts, categories, or cards in a file. When confronted with a stimulus, the child tried to "fit" the stimulus into an available schema. Thus the boy quite logically called the cow a dog, since for him, the characteristics of the cow closely approximated the characteristics of a dog. The cow met all the boy's criteria for a dog. The child's structures at this point did not permit him to perceive the differences between a cow and a dog, but he was able to see the similarities.[2]

At birth
→ *schemata reflexive*
→ *inferred from simple reflex motor activities*
→ *sucking/grasping*

Schemata are intellectual structures that organize events as they are perceived by the organism into groups according to common characteristics. They are repeatable psychological events in the sense that a child will repeatedly classify stimuli in a consistent manner. If a child "consistently" classifies cows as dogs, we can infer something about the nature of the child's concepts (schemata of cows and dogs).

At birth, schemata are reflexive in nature. That is, they can be inferred from simple reflex motor activities such as sucking and grasping. The sucking reflex illustrates a reflexive schema. At birth, infants typically suck on whatever is put in their mouths—a nipple, a finger—suggesting that there is no differentiation, that only a single, global sucking schema exists. Shortly after birth, infants learn to differentiate; when the infant is hungry, milk-producing stimuli are accepted and non-milk-producing stimuli are rejected. A differentiation exists at this point. In Piaget's words, the infant has two sucking schemata, one for milk-producing stimuli and one for non-milk-producing stimuli. At this time, schemata are not yet "mental" in the sense in which we usually think of the term. Schemata are reflexive. The infant makes real differentiations within his or her limited environment, but they are made via the reflexive and motor apparatus he or she has available. These differentiations on the most primitive level are the precursors of later "mental" activities.

As a child develops, schemata become more differentiated, less sensory, and more numerous; and the network they form becomes increasingly more complex. During early childhood, an infant has a few reflexive schemata that allow him or her to make a very few differentiations in the environment. An adult has a vast array of comparatively complex schemata that permit a great number of differentiations. The schemata of the adult evolve from the schemata of the child through adaptation and organization.

It is misleading to think that schemata do not change or that the young boy in our example is destined to call cows "dogs" for the rest of his life. Obviously, this does not happen. As a child becomes better able to generalize across stimuli, schemata become more refined.

At any point, a child's responses are assumed to reflect the nature of the child's concepts or schemata at that time. It is entirely "logical" for the boy described in the example to call a cow a "dog" when the schemata he has available are considered. Schemata are defined by (or reflected in) the overt behavior of the child. But schemata are more than the behavior; they are the internal structure from which the behavior flows. Behavior patterns that occur repeatedly in the course of cognitive activity are conceptualized as reflecting schemata. A schema subsumes a whole collection of distinct but similar action sequences. "Every schema is . . . coordinated with all other schemata and itself constitutes a totality with differentiated parts" (Piaget 1952c, p. 7).

Since schemata are structures of cognitive development that do change, allowance must be made for their growth and development. Adults' concepts are different from those of children. Concepts—schemata are their structural counterparts—change. The cognitive schemata of the adult are derived from the sensori-motor schemata of the child. The processes responsible for the change are *assimilation* and *accommodation.*

ASSIMILATION

Assimilation is the cognitive *process* by which a person integrates new perceptual, motor, or conceptual matter into existing schemata or patterns of behavior. One might say that a child has experiences: sees new things (cows) or sees old things in new ways, and hears things. The child tries to fit these new events or stimuli into the schemata he or she has at the time.[3] Suppose, as in the previous example, a boy is walking down a country road with his father, and the father points to a cow in the field and says, "What is that?" The child looks at the cow (stimulus) and says, "That's a dog." What has happened? The boy, seeing the object (cow) in the field, sifted through his collection of schemata until he found one that seemed appropriate and that could include the object. To the child, the object (cow) had all the characteristics of a dog—it fit into his dog schema—and so the child concluded that the object was a dog. The stimulus (cow) was assimilated into the dog schema. Thus assimilation can be viewed as the cognitive process of placing new stimulus events into existing schemata.

Assimilation goes on all the time. It would be an extreme oversimplification to suggest that a person processes one stimulus at a time. A human being must continually process an increasing number of stimuli.

Assimilation theoretically does not result in a change of schemata, but it does affect the growth of schemata and is thus a part of development. One might compare a schema to a balloon and assimilation to putting more air in the balloon. The balloon gets larger (assimilation growth), but it does not change its shape. Assimilation is a part of the process by which the individual cognitively adapts to and organizes the environment. The process of assimilation allows for the growth of schemata. It does not account for a change of schemata. We know schemata change. Adult schemata are different from those of children. Piaget accounted for the change of schemata with *accommodation*.

ACCOMMODATION

When confronted with a new stimulus, a child tries to assimilate it into existing schemata. Sometimes this is not possible. Sometimes a stimulus cannot be placed or assimilated into a schema because there are no schemata into which it readily fits. The characteristics of the stimulus do not approximate those required in any of the child's available schemata. What does the child do? Essentially he (or she) can do one of two things: (1) He can create a new schema into which he can place the stimulus (a new index card in the file), or (2) he can modify an existing schema so that the stimulus will fit into it. Both are forms of *accommodation*. Thus, accommodation is the creation of new schemata or the modification of old schemata. Both actions result in a change in, or development of, cognitive structures (schemata).

Once accommodation has taken place, a child can try again to assimilate the stimulus. Since the structure has

SOMETIMES YOU JUST HAVE TO ACCOMMODATE! (17)

changed, the stimulus is readily assimilated. Assimilation is always the end product.

The child who is actively assimilating and accommodating is in no way required or expected to evolve schemata that assume a particular form. Implicit in the conceptualizations of schema used here is the idea that schemata develop with experience over time. Schemata reflect the child's current level of understanding and knowledge of the world. The schemata have been *constructed* by the child. Since they are constructions, schemata are not accurate copies of reality. Their form is determined by assimilation and accommodation of experience, and over time they more closely approach reality in appearance. While the child is an infant, schemata are global—and, when compared to adults' schemata, extremely imprecise and frequently inaccurate. The processes of assimilation and accommodation that convert infants' rather primitive schemata into the more sophisticated adultlike schemata obviously take years.

During assimilation, a person imposes his or her available structure on the stimuli being processed. That is the stimuli are "forced" to fit the person's structure. In accommodation, the reverse is true. The person is "forced" to change his or her schema to fit the new stimuli. Accommodation accounts for development (a qualitative change), and assimilation accounts for growth (a quantitative change); together they account for intellectual adaptation and the development of intellectual structures.

EQUILIBRATION

The processes of assimilation and accommodation are necessary for cognitive growth and development. Of equal importance are the relative amounts of assimilation and accommodation that take place. For example, imagine the outcome in terms of mental development if a person always assimilated stimuli and never accommodated. Such a person would end up with a few very large schemata and would be unable to detect differences in things. Most things would be seen as similar. For John, the cow would forever remain a dog. On the other hand, what would be the result if a person always accommodated and never assimilated? It would result in a person having a great number of very small schemata that would have little generality. Most things would be seen as different. The person would be unable to detect similarities. Either of these extremes would result in abnormal intellectual growth. Therefore, a "balance" between assimilation and accommodation is as necessary as the processes themselves. (Piaget called the balance between assimilation and accommodation *equilibrium*. It is necessary to ensure the developing child's efficient interaction with the environment.)

Equilibrium is a state of balance between assimilation and accommodation. *Disequilibrium* is a state of imbalance between assimilation and accommodation.[4] *Equilibration* is the process of moving from disequilibrium to equilibrium. This is a self-regulatory *process* whose tools are assimilation and accommodation. Equilibration allows external experience to be incorporated into internal structures (schemata). When disequilibrium occurs, it provides motivation[5] for the child to seek equilibrium—to further assimilate or accommodate. Disequilibrium activates the process of equilibration and a striving to return to equilibrium. Equilibrium is a necessary condition toward which the organism constantly strives. The organism ultimately assimilates all stimuli (or stimulus events) with or without accommodation. This results in equilibrium. Thus, equilibrium can be viewed as a state of cognitive "balance" that is reached at the point of assimilation. Obviously, the equilibrium related to any particular stimulus may be a very temporary affair, as structures or schemata are constantly experiencing disequilibrium and change, but it is nonetheless important as development inches forward.

Everything must be assimilated by a child. The schemata the child uses may not be in harmony with those of adults (like classifying a cow as a dog), but the child's placement of stimuli into schemata is theoretically always appropriate for his or her level of conceptual development.

| MY SCHEMATA | MY SCHEMATA | MY SCHEMATA |
| Where can I put this? | Ah . . . ha . . .! | Love that equilibrium! |

There is no "wrong" placement. There are just better and better placements as intellectual development proceeds.

We can say, then, that the child, upon experiencing a new stimulus (or an old one again), tries to assimilate the stimulus into an existing schema. If he or she is successful, equilibrium is attained for the moment, relevant to the particular stimulus event. If the child cannot assimilate the stimulus, he or she then attempts to accommodate by modifying a schema or creating a new one. When this is done, assimilation of the stimulus proceeds, and equilibrium is reached for the moment.

Conceptually, cognitive growth and development proceed in this way at *all* levels of development. From birth through adulthood, knowledge is *constructed* by the individual, the schemata of adulthood being built (constructed) from the schemata of childhood. In assimilation, the organism "fits" stimuli into schemata that exist; in accommodation, the organism "changes" schemata to fit the stimulus. The process of accommodation results in a qualitative change in intellectual structures (schemata), while assimilation only adds to the existing structures—a quantitative change. Thus, assimilation and accommodation—a cumulative coordination, integration, and constant construction—account for the growth and development of cognitive structures and knowledge. Equilibration is the internal mechanism that regulates those processes. In the same sense that we adapt biologically to the world around us, the development of the mind—intellectual development—is also a process of adaptation.

NOTES

1. Constructs are concepts or "things" that are not directly observable but are inferred to exist (for example, intelligence, creativity, aptitude, ability, motivation, instincts). The list of constructs can be endless. A main activity of psychological research is to try to clarify the nature of constructs and verify their existence.

2. If we are concerned with the accuracy of John's response, we may be tempted to correct John and inform him that the animal is properly called a "cow" and that the response "dog" is incorrect. The result of this may well be confusion for John. John's response, "It's a dog," is a logical response given the configuration of schemata John has available at the time to think about the event. Thus, John's response is not wrong from his perspective—it is wrong only from an adult perspective. In addition, to be told that the proper name for the animal is "cow" may lead John to conclude that the things he calls dogs can be called either "dogs" or "cows." This is a logical inference to make.

3. Assimilation is a term Piaget borrowed from biology. It is the cognitive counterpart of eating, wherein food is eaten, digested, and assimilated, or changed into a usable form.

4. Disequilibrium can be thought of as "cognitive conflict" resulting when expectations or predictions are not confirmed by experience. A child expects something to happen in a certain way, and it does not. The discrepancy between the expected and what actually occurs is a form of disequilibrium.

5. Motivation can be thought of as that which activates behavior. In Piaget's theory, the major source of motivation with respect to intellectual development is disequilibrium. Disequilibrium activates equilibration (assimilation and accommodation).

<Chapter 2 >

COGNITIVE DEVELOPMENT AND OTHER FACTORS

CONTENT, FUNCTION, AND STRUCTURE

Piaget viewed intelligence as having three components: content, function, and structure. *Content* is what children know about. It refers to observable behaviors—sensori-motor and conceptual—that reflect intellectual activity. By its nature the content of intelligence varies considerably from age to age and from child to child. *Function* refers to those characteristics of intellectual activity—assimilation and accommodation—that are stable and continual throughout cognitive development. *Structure* refers to the inferred organizational properties (schemata) that explain the occurrence of particular behaviors. For example, if a child is asked to compare a row of 9 checkers to a longer row of 8 checkers and determine which has more checkers, and she says the row of 8 checkers has more, even though she counts each row, one can infer that she does not have a complete concept of number. This would suggest that her schema for number is not yet fully developed. When confronted with a problem that pits perception against *reason*, her choice is based on perception. Eventually *reason* will prevail, but only after the determining structures have changed. These changes in *structures* are intellectual development. Flavell writes:

> Interposed between function and content, Piaget postulates the existence of cognitive structures. Structure, like content and unlike function, does indeed change with age, and these developmental changes constitute the major object of study for Piaget. What are the structures in Piaget's system? They are the organizational properties of intelligence (schemata), organizations created through function and inferrable from the behavioral content whose nature they determine. (Flavell 1963, p. 17)

Piaget concerned himself primarily with the structure of intelligence, although he dealt with function and content to a lesser degree. His work involved the careful description and analysis of *qualitative* changes in development of these cognitive structures (schemata). Presumably, qualitative structural changes in cognitive functioning are most clearly changes in intellectual functioning—what is commonly called intelligence.[1]

ACTION AND KNOWLEDGE

Piaget's system requires that a child *act* in the environment if cognitive development is to proceed. The development of cognitive structures is ensured only if the child assimilates and accommodates stimuli in the environment. This can happen only if the child's senses are brought to bear on the environment. When the child is acting in the environment, moving in space, manipulating objects, searching with eyes and ears, or thinking, he or she is taking in the raw ingredients to be assimilated and accommodated. These actions result in the development of schemata.

STRUCTURE AND CONTENT CHANGE—FUNCTION DOES NOT

An infant cannot learn to differentiate between a nipple and an edge of the blanket unless he or she *acts* on both of them.

As the child becomes older, actions resulting in cognitive change become less overt. For the infant, the instrumental act may be movement of the arm and grasping. For the nine-year-old the instrumental act may be an internal one, as in adding a column of numbers. In both cases, the *activity* of the child is essential for development.

Actions necessary for cognitive development to occur are clearly more than just physical movement. Actions are behaviors that stimulate the child's intellectual apparatus, and they may or may not be observable. These behaviors produce disequilibrium and allow assimilation and accommodation to occur.

Mental and physical actions in the environment are a necessary but not sufficient condition for cognitive development. That is, the experience alone does not ensure development, but development cannot take place without it. Also necessary for development are assimilation and accommodation. Action is one of several interacting determinants of cognitive development.

For Piaget, all knowledge is a *construction* resulting from the child's actions. According to Piaget, there are three kinds of knowledge: physical knowledge, logical-mathematical knowledge, and social-arbitrary knowledge. Each requires the child's actions, but for different reasons.

Physical Knowledge: Discovery

Physical knowledge is knowledge of the physical properties of objects and events: size, shape, color, weight, and so forth. A child acquires physical knowledge about an object while manipulating (acting on) the object with his or her senses. For example, a young boy who is playing with sand may pour the sand from one container to another, feel it with his hands, or put it into his mouth. Through actions like these, children *discover* and construct their knowledge of sand. Active experiences are assimilated into schemata.

In the acquisition of physical knowledge, the objects themselves (for example, sand) "tell" the child what they can and cannot do. Feedback or reinforcement is provided by the objects themselves. The child cannot construct an accurate schemata of sand unless he acts on sand. Knowledge of objects cannot be acquired directly from reading, looking at pictures, or listening to what people say—these are all forms of symbolic representation—but only through actions on objects. Objects permit us to construct their properties only to the extent that we *act* on them (Wadsworth 1978).

Logical-Mathematical Knowledge: Invention

(Logical-mathematical knowledge is knowledge derived from thinking about experiences with objects and events (Gallagher and Reid 1981)[2] Like physical knowledge, logical-mathematical knowledge can develop only if a child acts on objects. But the respective roles of actions and objects in the construction of logical-mathematical knowledge are different. The child *invents* logical-mathematical knowledge; it is not inherent in objects, as physical knowledge is, but is constructed from the *actions* of the child on objects. The objects serve merely as a means of permitting the construction to occur.

Number concepts are examples of logical-mathematical concepts. We have all observed instances where children have been playing with sets of objects. A little girl may be playing with a set of 11 pennies. She puts them in a row and counts them. There are 11 of them. She puts them in a circle and counts them again. There are still 11 of them. The child stacks the pennies and counts them again. She counts 11 pennies. The child puts the pennies in a box and shakes them up. Removed from the box and counted, again there are 11 pennies. Through many active experiences like these, children eventually construct the concept or rule that the number of objects in a set remains the same regardless of the arrangement of the individual elements. The sum is independent of the order. This is an invention of logical-mathematical knowledge.

In the development of logical-mathematical knowledge, the nature of the objects is not critical, only that there are groups of objects for the child to manipulate. The concept the girl was developing in the preceding example could have developed as easily using stones, crayons, pots and pans, or flowers. As experiences are repeated over and over, in different settings and with different materials, these concepts become more refined. Like physical knowledge, logical-mathematical knowledge is not acquired from reading or listening to people talk. It is constructed from actions on objects.[3]

Social-Arbitrary Knowledge

Social-arbitrary knowledge is knowledge developed by humankind. It includes knowledge of rules, laws, morals, values, ethics, and language systems. This knowledge evolves within cultures. It cannot be extracted from actions on objects in the manner of physical and logical-mathematical knowledge. Social-arbitrary knowledge is constructed by children from their actions on (interactions with) other people. As children interact with each other and with adults, opportunities for the construction of social-arbitrary knowledge are encountered.[4]

According to Piagetian theory, all knowledge is physical knowledge, logical-mathematical knowledge, or social-

arbitrary knowledge (Wadsworth 1978). Of central importance in the construction of knowledge are the child's *actions* on objects and interactions with people. Knowledge cannot be derived directly from reading or from listening to people (for example, teachers) talk. Knowledge can be acquired only from *experience* with relevant objects; it cannot be acquired from representations (for example, written or spoken words) of objects and events. These are major implications for educational practice.

A child is more dependent on physical and sensorial experience in the early years of life when he or she does not possess the power of symbolic representation (language). At this time, interaction with the environment is primarily on a sensory and motor level. The child acts directly on objects in the environment. Development proceeds as the infant explores the environment via his or her reflexes. A variety of objects is placed in the mouth or sucked via the sucking reflex. Objects are grasped. These active reflexive behaviors allow the infant to construct his or her first differentiations within the environment. These actions allow the child to develop internal sensori-motor representations (schemata) of the objects as he or she makes discriminations.

As the typical child develops beyond age 2 or so, he or she becomes increasingly capable of representing action in the mind. The child's actions on the environment are mediated by internalized symbols and language and become less overt. Actions are less sensori-motor and more conceptual. Nonetheless, the active participation of the child remains necessary for cognitive development.

STAGES WITHIN THE CONTINUUM OF DEVELOPMENT

In the broadest sense, Piaget asserted throughout his work that cognitive and intellectual changes are the result of a developmental process. Piaget's general "hypothesis" is simply that cognitive development is a coherent process of successive qualitative changes of cognitive structures (schemata), each structure and its concomitant change deriving logically and inevitably from the preceding one. New schemata do not replace prior ones; they incorporate them, resulting in a qualitative change. If the young boy who classified a cow as a dog at some later time decides that the cow is no longer a dog but a new object called a "cow," he does not *replace* schemata. What he may do is create a new schema (accommodate) for cowlike objects, while retaining his old, but now modified, schema for dogs. Thus a change has occurred that results in a qualitatively superior set of schemata, the current schemata incorporating the previous ones.

Piaget conceptualized development as a continuous process along a continuum. Changes in intellectual development are gradual and never abrupt. Schemata are constructed and reconstructed (or modified) gradually. From a Piagetian perspective, development is appropriately viewed as a continuum. For purposes of conceptualizing cognitive growth, intellectual development can be divided into four broad stages (and other periods and substages).[5]

Piaget was criticized for the use of stages in his theory. Those who objected to his use of stages *probably* did so out of a misunderstanding. Piaget did not suggest that children move from discrete stage to discrete stage in development as one moves from one step to another while walking upstairs. Cognitive development flows along, but the defining stage is useful to the observer in conceptualizing the developmental process. The researcher and theorist can divide the long period of development into periods of shorter length; thus, development can be analyzed and, in some ways, conceptualized more efficiently. This does not in any way deny the continuity of development over its entire course, nor does it mean that the stages are selected without a rationale.

Piaget broadly summarized the stages of cognitive development as:

1. *The stage of sensori-motor intelligence (0-2 years).* During this stage, behavior is primarily motor. The child does not yet internally represent events and "think" conceptually, though "cognitive" development is seen as schemata are constructed.

2. *The stage of preoperational thought (2-7 years).* This

stage is characterized by the development of language and other forms of representation and rapid conceptual development. Reasoning during this stage is prelogical or semilogical.

3. *The stage of concrete operations (7-11 years).* During these years, the child develops the ability to apply logical thought to concrete problems.

4. *The stage of formal operations (11-15 years or older).* During this stage, the child's cognitive *structures* reach their greatest level of development, and the child becomes able to apply logical reasoning to all classes of problems. (Piaget 1963b)

Development is thought to flow along in a cumulative manner, each new step in development built upon and becoming integrated with previous steps. The behaviors described are only typical behaviors of a given age, period, or stage.

> In a general way, the fact should be emphasized that the behavior patterns characteristic of the different stages do not succeed each other in a linear way (those of a given stage disappearing at the time when those of the following one take form) but in the manner of the layers of a pyramid (upright, or upside down), the new behavior patterns simply being added to the old ones to complete, correct, or combine with them. (Piaget 1952c, p. 329)

The chronological ages during which children can be expected to develop behavior representative of a particular stage are not fixed. The age spans suggested by Piaget are normative and denote the times during which a typical or average child can be expected to display the intellectual behaviors that are characteristic of the particular stage. The typical child enters the preoperational stage around age 2. Although some enter the stage earlier—a very small percentage of one-year-olds enter the preoperational stage— other children do not enter the preoperational stage until age 3 or 4. With severely "retarded" or developmentally delayed children, development may be even slower.

The behaviors that will be described for each stage are *only* typical for the age groups. The norms established by Piaget are for samples of children in Geneva and do not necessarily hold rigidly for American or other samples. Piaget assumed that the fixed order of appearance (of structures of behavior) implies nothing concerning the experiential or hereditary basis for the order. The age at which the stages occur can vary with the nature of both an individual's experience and his or her hereditary potential (ibid., p. 255). Progress through stages is not automatic (as in maturation theory).

One aspect of Piaget's theory is "fixed." According to Piaget, every child *must* pass through the stages of cognitive development in the same order. A child cannot move intellectually from the preoperational stage to the stage of formal operations without passing through the stage of concrete operations.

Nevertheless, the rates at which children pass through the stages may not be identical because of experiential or hereditary factors. "Bright" children may go through the stages rapidly; "dull" children may progress more slowly, some never reaching or completing the last stage (formal operations).

Although a concept of stages of intellectual development is used, it should be remembered that the range of intellectual behaviors within a particular stage is large. That is, while the child develops the use of language during the preoperational stage (2–7 years), it is expected that language usage at age 7 will be qualitatively different than at age 2.

In the early part of the preoperational stage, language ability is formed and organized. Thus, the language behaviors of the three-year-old typically lack the organization and stability of those of the seven-year-old, though they will both demonstrate characteristics of the stage. Thus, behaviors early in a stage, or early in the development of a particular intellectual function, can be expected to have less stability and to be less sophisticated than behaviors in later periods.

FACTORS IN DEVELOPMENT

We have seen that mental development follows a "fixed" course along a continuum. From birth through adulthood, the structures of intelligence, schemata, are constantly developing as the child spontaneously acts on the environment and assimilates and accommodates to an increasing array of stimuli in the environment. For purposes of analysis, the continuum of development is divided into the four stages indicated earlier. The roles of active experience (assimilation and accommodation) and equilibration (self-regulation) as agents in development have been discussed in part. Before proceeding to a discussion of each stage within the continuum, let us consider in some detail the four factors of development, and the *relationship* of the four factors.

Piaget suggested four broad factors that are related to all cognitive development: (1) maturation, (2) physical experience, (3) social interaction, and (4) a general progression of equilibrium (Piaget 1961, p. 277). He viewed each of these factors and their *interaction* as necessary conditions for cognitive development, but none alone is sufficient to ensure cognitive development. Movement within and between stages of development is a function of these factors and their interaction.

Maturation and Heredity

Piaget believed that heredity plays a role in cognitive development, though heredity alone cannot account for intellectual development. He asserted that heredity sets limits for development at any point in time. Maturation, the (rate of) unfolding of inherited potential, is the mechanism through which these limits are established. Flavell writes:

> . . . maturation as regards cognitive functions—knowledge—simply determines the range of possibilities at a specific stage. It does not cause the actualization of the structures. Maturation simply indicates

whether or not the construction of specific structures
is possible at a specific stage. It does not itself contain a preformed structure, but simply opens up possibilities. The new reality still has to be constructed.
(Flavell 1971, p. 193)

Thus, maturation factors (or inherited factors) place
broad constraints on cognitive development. These constraints change as maturation proceeds. Realization of the
"potential" implied by these constraints at any point in
development depends on a child's actions on his or her
environment.

Active Experience

Earlier in this chapter we discussed the importance of
children's actions on the environment. Active experience is
one of the four factors in cognitive development. Each kind
of knowledge a child constructs—physical knowledge, logical-mathematical knowledge, and social-arbitrary knowledge—requires him or her to interact with objects or people. Actions may be physical manipulations of objects or
events or mental manipulations of objects or events (thinking). Active experiences are those that provoke assimilation
and accommodation, resulting in cognitive change (change
in structures or schemata).

Social Interaction

Another factor in cognitive development is social
interaction. By social interaction, Piaget meant the interchange of ideas among people. This, as we have seen, is
particularly important in the development of social-arbitrary knowledge. The concepts or schemata that people
develop can be classified as follows: (1) those that have sen-
sorially available physical referents (they can be seen, heard,
and so on), and (2) those that do not have such referents.
The concept *tree* has physical referents; the concept *honesty*
does not. A child can develop a socially acceptable concept

of *tree* (physical knowledge) relatively independent of others because referents (trees) are usually available. But the same child cannot develop an acceptable concept of *honesty* (social-arbitrary knowledge) independent of others. To the extent that concepts are "arbitrary," or socially defined, the child is dependent on social interaction for the construction and validation of concepts.

Interaction with others can also serve to provoke disequilibrim relative to physical and logical-mathematical knowledge. When children are in situations where their thinking conflicts with that of other children (or adults), the conflict can be instrumental in leading them to question their own thinking (disequilibrium). As we see later, conflicts in thought can result in disequilibrium but do not automatically do so.

Social interaction can be of many kinds. One interacts with peers, parents, and other adults. The events that take place in the schoolroom are most frequently the interaction of students with other students and with their teachers. There is also the interaction with parents and others in the environment. All these interactions are important in cognitive development.

Equilibration

Maturation, experience, and social interaction do not sufficiently explain cognitive development. Piaget's remaining factor is *equilibration*.

> It seems to me there are two reasons for having to call in this fourth factor (equilibration). The first is that since we already have three other factors, there must be some kind of coordination among them. This coordination is a kind of equilibration. Secondly, in . . . construction . . . a subject goes through much trial and error and many regulations that in large part involve self-regulations. Self-regulations are the very nature of equilibration. (Piaget 1977a, p. 10)

⅄   (In this way, Piaget used the concept of equilibration to explain the coordination of other factors and the regulation of development in general.)As children have experiences, construction occurs. Coordination of existing knowledge with the new knowledge occurs (assimilation and accommodation). There is a general internal monitoring and regulating of this system. Equilibration is the regulator

⅄   that allows new experience to be successfully incorporated into schemata.)

The control of development is in large part internal. Piaget viewed this as a *self-regulatory* process, with equilibration the mechanism for self-regulation.

Affective Development

The discussion of Piaget's theory and work to this point has focused exclusively on cognitive and intellectual development. A second major aspect of development is affective development. Affect is concerned with emotions, values, moral reasoning, and "feelings." People frequently view affect and intelligence as separate functions within an individual. In Piaget's view, this separation is largely unjustified, although it is certainly legitimate to conceptualize them as separate for purposes of analysis.

Many people believe that the affective aspects of human life arise from some internal source in a more or less predetermined form. Piaget believed that affect is no more preformed than is intelligence. In Piaget's view there are remarkable parallels between the cognitive and affective. First, affect *develops* in the same sense that cognition or intelligence develops. When we examine children's reasoning about moral questions, one aspect of affective life, we see that children's moral concepts are constructed in the same sense that cognitive concepts are constructed. The preschool or early elementary child who is accidentally bumped by another child usually does not view the incident as an "accident," largely because he or she has not yet constructed concepts of intentionality. Similarly, we shall see that more or less permanent personality characteristics do not usually emerge until adolescence (Piaget 1981). As intelligence is developing, there is a parallel affective development. The mechanisms for construction are the same. Children assimilate experience to affective schemata in the same way they assimilate experience to cognitive structures. The outcome is knowledge.

Piaget also argued that *all* behavior has both affective and cognitive aspects. There is no pure cognitive behavior and no pure affective behavior. The child who "likes" mathematics typically makes rapid progress. The child who "dislikes" mathematics typically does not make rapid progress. The cognitive behavior in each case is influenced by affect. "It is impossible to find behavior arising from affectivity alone without any cognitive element. It is equally impossible to find behavior composed only of cognitive elements" (ibid., p. 2).

The interplay of cognitive and affective aspects of thought and knowledge can be observed in children's moral concepts.

SUMMARY

Piaget viewed intelligence as having three components: content, function, and structure. He identified three kinds of knowledge: physical knowledge, logical-mathematical knowledge, and social-arbitrary knowledge. Physical knowledge is knowledge of properties of objects and is derived from actions on objects. Logical-mathematical knowledge is knowledge constructed from *actions* on objects. Social-arbitrary knowledge is knowledge about things created by cultures. Each kind of knowledge depends on actions, physical or mental. Actions instrumental in development are those that generate disequilibrium and lead to efforts to reestablish equilibrium (equilibration). Assimilation and accommodation are the agents of equilibration, the self-regulator of development.

Four factors and their interaction are necessary for development: maturation, active experience, social interaction, and equilibration. Cognitive development, while a continuous process, can be divided into four stages for purposes of analysis and description. Affective development (emotions and feelings) evolves in a manner similar to cognitive development. That is, affective structures are constructed as cognitive structures are constructed.

NOTES

1. It should be noted that most "intelligence" tests to a large extent sample cognitive content, and to a lesser extent cognitive structure. By and large, they are quantitative measures, not qualitative. Piaget's conceptualizations suggest that "intelligence" tests should measure cognitive structures as well as content if development is to be assessed accurately.

2. I have chosen to use the term *logical*-mathematical knowledge whereas Piaget and most of those writing about Piaget's work use the term *logico*-mathematical.

3. Kamii indicates that all logical-mathematical knowledge involves construction of *relationships*.

> When . . . we are presented with a red chip and a blue one, and note that they are different, the difference is an example of logico-mathematical knowledge. The chips are indeed observable, but the difference between them is not. The difference is a *relationship* created mentally by the individual who puts the two objects into a relationship. (1982, p. 7)

4. Chapters 3 through 6 deal in some depth with the development of moral concepts within the context of affective development. Moral concepts are examples of social-arbitrary knowledge.

5. The number of stages one divides development into is somewhat arbitrary. On different occasions Piaget divided development into three, four, or six major stages, each time with a number of substages. I have divided development into four stages.

Chapter 3

THE SENSORI-MOTOR STAGE

Mental development is a process that begins the day an infant is born (and possibly sooner). This does not mean that the child is born thinking (internally representing objects in the mind), but it does mean that the sensori-motor behaviors that occur from birth onward are necessary for, and instrumental in, later cognitive development. To look at it another way, intellectual behavior at any age evolves directly from prior levels of behavior. Thus, the roots of all intellectual development are in early sensori-motor behavior.

In several of his books Piaget carefully described intellectual and affective development during the first two years of life. From his observations and writings, it is clear that the structures of intelligence and feelings begin to evolve during infancy. At birth, an infant can perform only simple reflex behaviors. Two years after birth, the child is typically beginning to talk (symbolic representation) and has clearly evolved intellectual operations and is beginning to "think." Through internal representation, the two-year-old typically can mentally "invent" means (behaviors) that will permit him or her to do things (attain ends). The child can solve most sensori-motor problems; that is, he or she can get the objects wanted by using one object to retrieve another. At birth and for the first month of life, affect is seen only in undifferentiated reflex activity. Initially there are no true "feelings" or differentiated affective reactions. During the sensori-motor stage feelings develop, and by the end of the stage, children's affective feelings begin to play a role in the selection of actions.

The two-year-old is cognitively and affectively different from the newborn infant. At age 2 the child has a comparatively much larger and more sophisticated array of cognitive and affective schemata. The evolution that occurs is primarily a function of the child's sensori-motor actions on the environment, resulting in ongoing assimilation and accommodation that in turn result in qualitative and quantitative changes in schemata.

> The period that extends from birth to the acquisition of language is marked by an extraordinary development of the mind. Its importance is sometimes underestimated because it is not accompanied by words that permit a step-by-step pursuit of the progress of intelligence and the emotions, as is the case later on. This early mental development nonetheless determines the entire course of psychological evolution. . . . At the starting point of this development the neonate grasps everything to himself—or, in more precise terms, to his own body—whereas at the termination of the period, i.e., when language and thought begin, he is for all practical purposes but one element or entity among others in a universe that he has gradually constructed himself, and which hereafter he will experience as external to himself. (Piaget 1967, pp. 8–9)

To understand that the development of language in the two-year-old is related to earlier sensori-motor development, the observer must carefully observe behavior during the first two years of life. The evolution that occurs is a remarkably smooth succession of periods, each incorporating the previous period, each marking a new advance.

Piaget divided the sensori-motor stage into six periods in which progressively more complex patterns of intellectual behavior evolve (see Table 3.1). The remainder of this chapter presents aspects of the six periods of sensori-motor development. The general characteristics of each period are discussed. These include the progressive development of a child's *object* concept and his or her concept of *causality*, two of the most important indicators of intellectual and affective development during this stage.

What has previously been said about stages of development applies equally well to the periods of development about to be discussed. As behaviors evolve that are representative of a more advanced stage, the behaviors of previous stages are not totally displaced. Old, less sophisticated behaviors still occur. Regarding new stages, Piaget wrote:

> The new stage would thus be defined by the fact that the child becomes capable of certain behavior patterns of which he was up to then incapable; it is not the fact that he renounces the behavior patterns of the preceding stages, even if they are contrary to the new ones or contradictory to them from the observer's point of view. (Piaget 1964, p. 299)

PERIOD 1 (0–1 MONTH)

Beginning at birth and throughout most of the first period of sensori-motor development, the behavior of a typical infant is entirely reflexive. The basic reflexes that the infant is born with are sucking, grasping, crying, and movement of the arms, trunk, and head. When an infant is stimulated, his (or her) reflexes respond. Thus, when an object is put in the infant's mouth, he sucks on it, regardless of what it is. When an object contacts the palm of the infant's hand, he grasps it, regardless of what it is. There is no evidence that the infant, behaving so, can differentiate between objects. His reflex responses are more or less the same to all objects. A blanket is sucked on as vigorously as a milk-producing nipple. The hand grasps what comes into it, be it someone's finger or a toy. No distinction is made between stimuli. Thus, during this period, the infant *assimilates* all stimuli through the reflex systems. At birth, all stimulus

Table 3.1

Characteristics of Development during the Sensori-Motor Stage

Period	General	Object Concept	Space	Causality	Affect
1 Reflex, 0–1 mo.	Reflex activity	No differentiation of self from other objects	Egocentric	Egocentric	Instinctual drives and inborn affective reactions
2 First differentiations, 1–4 mos.	Hand-mouth coordination; differentiation via sucking, grasping	No special behavior re vanished objects; no differentiation of movement of self and external objects	Changes in perspective seen as changes in objects	No differentiation of movement of self and external objects	First acquired feelings (joy, sorrow, pleasantness, unpleasantness. Feelings of contentment and disappointment linked to action
3 Reproduction, 4–8 mos.	Eye-hand coordination; reproduction of interesting events	Anticipates positions of moving objects	Space externalized; no spatial relationships of objects	Self seen as cause of all events	

	Coordination of schemata	Object permanence	Perceptual constancy of size and shape of objects	Elementary externalization of causality	Affect
4 Coordination of schemata, 8–12 mos.	Coordination of schemata; application of known means to new problems; anticipation	Object permanence; searches for vanished objects; reverses bottle to get nipple	Perceptual constancy of size and shape of objects	Elementary externalization of causality	Affect involved in activation and retardation or intention or intentional actions. First feelings of success or failure. Investment of affection in others
5 Experimentation, 12–18 mos.	Discovery of new means through experimentation	Considers sequential displacements while searching for vanished objects	Aware of relationships between objects in space, between objects and self	Self seen as object among objects and self as object of actions	
6 Representation, 18–24 mos.	Representation; invention of new means via internal combinations	Images of absent objects, representation of displacements	Aware of movements not perceived; representation of spatial relationships	Representative causality; causes and effects inferred	

Source: Adapted from Wadsworth 1979; Piaget 1981.

events are incorporated (assimilated) into primitive reflexive *schemata* in an undifferentiated manner.

Within a few weeks of birth, simple *accommodations* on the part of the child are usually observable. At birth the infant sucks on what is placed in his mouth. A nipple is sucked on when presented. Soon the infant begins to "search" for the nipple if it cannot be found; in effect, accommodating to the environment. The infant's "searching" is a behavior that was not present at birth and cannot be attributed to any reflex system. There is no "searching" reflex; there is only a sucking reflex. Thus, the active searching is a change in reflex behavior on the part of the infant—an *accommodation*.

The innate, random reflex acts observable during the first period undergo modification as a result of their repetitive use and interaction with the environment. While the young infant seems to be only exercising his reflexes when behaving, and no intellectual behaviors are observable, the *use* of the reflexes is essential for development during the stage and for the development of cognitive structures that are to follow. From the beginning, acts of assimilation and accommodation are present.

Object Concept

One of Piaget's important beliefs was that all concepts, including the object concept, are developed and are not innate. That is, the awareness that objects are more or less permanent and are not destroyed when they disappear is not an inherited characteristic. This awareness of objects is developed out of sensori-motor experiences little by little (Piaget 1954, p. 4). In effect, a child must construct the universe of objects through experiences. At birth an infant has no awareness of objects other than on a reflexive level. Indeed, the infant is unable to differentiate between the self and the environment. The infant has no concept of objects. Any object presented by the external environment is merely something to suck, to grasp, or to look at—something that evokes an undifferentiated reflexive response.

Concept of Causality

Causality, an awareness of cause-and-effect relationships, is another important concept that develops during the sensori-motor stage. At birth the child is totally egocentric[1] and is not aware of causality at all. Not until later does awareness of causality begin to evolve.

Affect

This first period is one of reflexes and instinctual drives (Piaget 1981). Newborns seek nourishment and relief from discomfort—with their reflexes determining behavior. They suck and they cry. During this period, there are no "feelings" as such. All affect is associated with reflexes.

PERIOD 2 (1–4 MONTHS)

The second period of sensori-motor development begins when the reflexive behaviors of the previous period begin to be modified. During this period, several new behaviors appear. Thumb-sucking frequently becomes habitual and reflects the development of some hand-mouth coordination; moving objects are followed with the eyes (eye coordination); and the head is moved in the direction of sounds (eye-ear coordination).

Early in Period 1, an infant's responses to stimuli are purely reflexive. No differentiation is initially made between stimuli. Toward the end of Period 1, an infant begins to distinguish between objects, a behavior not present at birth. For example, the infant actively sucks on a milk-producing nipple (when hungry), but rejects other objects placed in her mouth if she wants milk. A reflex has been modified, indicating that the infant has made an *accommodation* to the environment. Where a primitive sucking *schema* that did not permit differentiation existed, a more sophisticated schema permitting differentiation now exists. Changes in behavior such as this are the first observable, if primitive, signs of the internal organization of, and adaptation to, the environment.

Habitual thumb-sucking is a behavior typically acquired during this period (Piaget 1952c, p. 48). This new behavior requires hand-mouth coordination, an ability that the infant does not have during the first month. Prior to this time, the thumb-sucking that occurs is usually a random or chance occurrence; the thumb happens to get into the mouth. Habituation of the activity cannot be explained by reflexes alone. It can be explained only by a child's construction of elementary sensori-motor relationships from his or her actions.

Piaget illustrates the transition from random to clearly coordinated thumb-sucking:

Observation 19. At 0;1(4)[2] after the 6 P.M. meal Laurent is wide awake (as was not the case at the preceding meals) and not completely satisfied. First he makes vigorous sucking-like movements, then his right hand may be seen approaching his mouth, touching his lower lip and finally being grasped. But as only the index finger was grasped, the hand fell out again. Shortly afterward it returned. This time the thumb was in the mouth while the index finger was placed between the gums and the upper lip. The hand then moves 5 cm. away from the mouth only to reenter it; now the thumb is grasped and the other fingers remain outside. Laurent then is motionless and sucks vigorously, drooling so much that after a few moments he is removed. A fourth time the hand approaches and three fingers enter the mouth. The hand leaves again and reenters a fifth time. As the thumb has again been grasped, sucking is resumed. I then remove the hand and place it near his waist. Laurent seems to give up sucking and gazes ahead, contented and satisfied. But after a few minutes the lips move and the hand approaches them again. This time there is a series of setbacks; the fingers are placed on the chin and lower lip. The index finger enters the mouth twice (consequently the sixth and seventh time this has succeeded). The eighth time

the hand enters the mouth, the thumb alone is
retained and sucking continues. I again remove the
hand. Again lip movements cease, new attempts
ensue, success results for the ninth and tenth time,
after which the experiment is interrupted. (Ibid.,
p. 53)

Laurent's thumb-sucking is rapidly becoming habitual. Since it is directed by the child, the behavior is different from all reflex behavior at birth. Such coordination
implies an *accommodation* on the part of the child.

On the matter of thumb-sucking, Piaget wrote:

When the child systematically sucks his thumb,
no longer due to chance contacts but through coordination between hand and mouth, this may be called
acquired accommodation. Neither the reflexes of the
mouth nor of the hand can be provided such coordination by heredity (there is no instinct to suck the
thumb!) and experience alone explains its formation.
(Ibid., p. 48)

During the second period, coordinations develop in
the use of the eyes. The child begins to follow moving objects
with his or her eyes. Piaget provided an example:

Observation 28.—Jacqueline at 0;0(16) does not
follow with her eyes the flame of a match 20 cm.
away. Only her expression changes at the sight of it
and then she moves her head as though to find the
light again. She does not succeed despite the dim
light in the room. At 0;0(24), on the other hand, she
follows the match perfectly under the same conditions. The subsequent days her eyes follow the movements of my hand, a moving handkerchief, etc.
(Ibid., p. 63)

The ability to visually follow moving objects is not
present at birth. As can be seen in Jacqueline's case, this
ability is acquired.

Coordination between hearing and vision begins to develop at this time. Discriminations between sounds also begin to occur. This is evident when children begin to move their heads in the direction of sounds, and when faces of people are clearly associated with sounds by the same person.

> Observation 48.—From 0;1(26), on the other hand, Laurent turns to the right direction as soon as he hears my voice (even if he has not seen me just before) and seems satisfied when he has discovered my face even when it is immobile. At 0;1(27) he looks successively at his father, his mother, and again at his father after hearing my voice. It therefore seems that he ascribes this voice to a visually familiar face. At 0;2(14) he observes Jacqueline at 1.90 to 2 meters, at the sound of her voice; same observation at 0;2(21). At 0;3(1) I squat before him while he is in his mother's arms and I make the sound *bzz* (which he likes). He looks to his left, then to his right, then ahead, then below him; then he catches sight of my hair and lowers his eyes until he sees my motionless face. Finally he smiles. This last observation may be considered as definitely indicating identification of the voice and visual image of the person.
>
> These examples illustrate some of the cognitive differences between a typical child during the first two periods. The younger child makes undifferentiated reflex responses to stimuli. The older child makes primitive sensori-motor differentiations and acquires limited sensori-motor coordinations. This development of schemata comes about as the infant acts using his reflexes, assimilating and accommodating experience. (Ibid., pp. 82–83)

Object Concept

During the second period of sensori-motor development, the child evokes an awareness of objects that was not present during the first period. As before, the child tries to look at the objects she (or he) hears, indicating a coordination between vision and hearing. In addition, the child may continue to follow the path of an object with her eyes after it has disappeared from view. The following example from Piaget illustrates acquired visual following:

> Thus, Lucienne, at 0;3(9), sees me at the extreme left of her visual field and smiles vaguely. She looks in different directions, in front of her and to the right, but constantly returns to the place in which she sees me and dwells on it every time for a moment. . . .
>
> At 0;4(26) she takes the breast but turns when I call her and smiles at me. Then she resumes nursing but several times in succession, despite my silence, she turns directly to the position from which she can see me. She does it again after a pause of a few minutes. Then I withdraw; when she turns without finding me her expression is one of mingled disappointment and expectation. (Piaget 1954, pp. 10–11)

Lucienne (one of Piaget's daughters) demonstrates clearly that she has coordination between hearing and vision. She locates visually the source of sounds. In addition, she is able to return and visually locate objects that have left her field of vision.

Intentionality

A number of new sensori-motor coordinations develop in Period 2. An infant's range of responses increases. Although advances have been made, a child's behavior still lacks *intention* in the sense that he or she initiates behaviors directed at certain ends. Behaviors are still primarily reflexive (though modified), and goals are set off only *after* behavior sequences are begun.

> As long as action is entirely determined by directly perceived sensorial images, there can be no question of intention. Even when the child grasps an object in order to look at it, one cannot infer that there is a conscious purpose. It is with the appearance of . . . deferred reactions that the purpose of the action, ceasing to be in some way directly perceived,

presupposes a continuity in searching, and consequently a beginning of intention. (Piaget 1952c,
p. 143)

Intentionality of behavior can be inferred only when the
initiation of behaviors is not a reflex act or a simple repetition of preceding behavior.

Thus, the initial steps in intellectual development have
begun. The child's actions in the environment, resulting in
assimilations and accommodations, have produced primitive structural changes permitting simple sensori-motor
coordinations. In the next period these advances are elaborated and surpassed through the same processes.

Affect—Acquired Feelings

According to Piaget, two kinds of feelings make their
appearance during this period and the next.

To begin with, *perceptual affects* make their
appearance. These are feelings such as pleasure,
pain, pleasantness, unpleasantness, etc., that have
become attached to perceptions through experience.
The second development is the differentiation of
needs and interests. This has to do with *feelings* of
contentment, disappointment, and all gradations in
between that are not just tied to various perceptions
but that are *associated with action as a whole*. (Piaget
1981, p. 21)

General states of global tension and relaxation are
observed during these periods.

During the second period of sensori-motor development, affect remains totally invested in one's own activities
and body. In Piaget's view, the reason that affect is not yet
"transferred" to others is that the infant, at this point in
development, has not yet differentiated the self as an object
from other objects in the environment. The self and the
environment are still one. Thus the infant's body continues
to remain the focus of all activity and affect.

PERIOD 3 (4–8 MONTHS)

During Period 3, the child's behaviors become increasingly oriented toward objects and events beyond his or her own body. For example, a child grasps and manipulates objects she can reach, signifying coordination between vision and tactile senses. Prior to this time, the infant's behavior has been oriented primarily toward herself. She has been unable to effectively distinguish herself from other objects on a sensori-motor level. She has been unable to coordinate the movement of her hands with her eyes.

Another characteristic of the third period is that infants reproduce events that occur that are of interest to them. When interesting experiences occur, they try to repeat them. A cord attached to overhead bells is pulled repeatedly. Grasping and striking acts are repeated intentionally. There are clear attempts to sustain and repeat acts. Piaget referred to these phenomena as *circulator reactions*[3] or *reproductive assimilation*. The infant tries to reproduce events that are of interest to him or her. To illustrate:

> Observation 104.—At 0;3(29) Laurent grasps a paper knife which he sees for the first time; he looks at it a moment and then swings it while holding it in his right hand. During these movements the object happens to rub against the wicker of the bassinet. Laurent then waves his arms vigorously and obviously tries to reproduce the sound he has heard, but without understanding the necessity of contact between the paper and the wicker and, consequently, without achieving this contact otherwise than by chance.
>
> At 0;4(3) same reactions, but Laurent looks at the object at the time when it happens to rub against the wicker of the bassinet. The same still occurs at 0;4(5) but there is slight progress towards systemization.
>
> Finally at 0;4(6) the movement becomes intentional; as soon as the child has the object in his hand he rubs it with regularity against the wicker of the bassinet. (Piaget 1981, pp. 168–69)

When a child successfully repeats previous behaviors, as Laurent did in the example, primitive sensori-motor intentionality is evident. These *circular reactions* are clear examples of active interactions with the environment. They are a form of assimilation that represents an advance over earlier assimilation.

Intentionality

One characteristic of the sensori-motor stage is the child's progress from nonintentional behavior to a form of intentional behavior. During the second period of sensori-motor development, intentional behavior is not evident. At that time behavior is random and is elicited by stimulation. Actions are not designed to attain a goal or object. During Period 3, a child begins to engage in a goal-directed (intentional) behavior. He or she tries to repeat unusual and interesting events. In Period 3, goals are established only *after* behaviors have begun. The infant's goals become established only during the repetitions of behaviors; consequently, the intentionality (goal direction) is after the fact, so to speak, after behavior has begun. In later sensori-motor periods (Period 4), the infant *initiates* a behavior sequence with a goal to be attained already in mind, and selects means that he or she thinks will attain the goal. Intentionality is present at the beginning of the sequence, and thus the behavior is not a mere repetition of a previous behavior but an intentional act. While behavior in Period 3 is for the first time intentional, it is not intentional until after behavior sequences have begun.

Object Concept

During Period 3, a child begins to anticipate the positions that objects will pass through while they are moving. This indicates development of the child's awareness of the permanence of objects. To illustrate:

> Observation 6.—Laurent's reaction to falling
> objects still seems to be nonexistent at 0;5(24): he

does not follow with his eyes any of the objects which I drop in front of him.

At 0;5(30) no reaction to the fall of a box of matches. The same is true at 0;6(0), but when he drops the box himself he searches for it next to him with his eyes (he is lying down).

At 0;6(7) he holds an empty match box in his hand. When it falls his eyes search for it even if they have not followed the beginning of the fall; he turns his head in order to see it on the sheet. Same reaction at 0;6(9) with a rattle.

At 0;7(29) he searches on the floor for everything I drop above him, if he has in the least perceived the beginning of the movement of falling. (Piaget 1954, pp. 14–15)

In the example, Laurent by 8 months of age is looking for objects in places where he predicts they have fallen. He is anticipating the positions falling objects will assume, demonstrating a more sophisticated schema of object than in previous stages.

Concept of Causality

During Period 3, a child remains egocentric. The child sees himself or herself as the primary cause of all activity. The following example illustrates the child's egocentric awareness of causality during Period 3.

At 0;7(8) Laurent is seated and I place a large cushion within his reach. I scratch the cushion. He laughs. Afterward I move my hand five cm. from the cushion, between it and his own hands, in such a way that if he pushed it slightly it would press against the cushion. As soon as I pause, Laurent strikes the cushion, arches, swings his head, etc. True, subsequently he does sometimes grasp my hand. But it is only in order to strike it, shake it, etc., and he does not once try to move it forward or put it in contact with the cushion.

At a certain moment he scratches my hand; on the other hand, he does not scratch the cushion

although this behavior is familiar to him. (Ibid.,
p. 245)

Clearly, Laurent believes he alone can cause events.
He is not aware that his father's hand is causing the interesting sound when it is in contact with the cushion. He
shakes his father's hand to make the sound; he scratches
the hand. He acts on the hand and on the cushion, but never
on the two together. The child at this period sees himself
as the cause of all events.

PERIOD 4 (8–12 MONTHS)

Toward the end of the first year of life, behavior patterns emerge that constitute clear acts of intelligence. The
infant begins to use means to attain ends. "The child has
the ability to combine behaviors he previously acquired in
order to achieve goals" (Piaget 1981). The child begins to
anticipate events, demonstrating prevision. Objects take on
a noticeable measure of permanence for the child. For
example, she begins to search for objects that she sees disappear. Also, she comes to see that other objects in the environment can be sources of activity (causality).

Prior to this period, behavior has always been a direct
action of the child on objects. Interesting acts are prolonged
or repeated. That is, a single *schema* had been used to evoke
a behavioral response. During Period 4, the child begins to
coordinate two familiar schemata in generating a single
act; she begins to use means to attain ends that are not
immediately attainable in a direct way. Children can be
seen to set aside one object (means) to get to another object
(end). A pillow is moved out of the way to reach a toy. There
is an *intentional* selection of means prior to the initiation
of behavior. The end is established from the beginning, the
means being used precisely in order to reach the end. The
following illustrates the means-ends coordination that
develops:

Observation 121.—At 0:8(20) Jacqueline tries to
grasp a cigarette case which I present to her. I then

slide it between the crossed strings which attach her
dolls to the hood (of her bassinet). She tries to reach
it directly. Not succeeding, she immediately looks for
the strings which are not in her hands and of which
she only saw the part in which the cigarette case is
entangled. She looks in front of her, grasps the
strings, pulls and shakes them, etc. The cigarette
case then falls and she grasps it.

Second experiment: same reaction, but without
first trying to grasp the object directly. (Piaget 1952c,
p. 215)

In the example Jacqueline pulls the strings (means) to
attain the cigarette case (end). Clearly this is an intentional
act from the outset. Means and ends (two schemata) are
coordinated in one action.

During Period 4, the infant shows clear signs of event
anticipation. Certain "signs" are recognized as being associated with certain actions that follow the signs. These actions
illustrate prevision and the "meaning" of certain events.

Observation 132.—At 0;8(6) Laurent recognizes
by a certain noise caused by air that he is nearing
the end of his feeding and, instead of insisting on
drinking to the last drop, he rejects his bottle.

Observation 133.—At 0;9(15) Jacqueline wails
or cries when she sees the person seated next to her
get up or move away a little (giving the impression
of leaving).

At 1;1(10) she has a slight scratch which is disin-
fected with alcohol. She cries, chiefly from fear. Subsequently, as soon as she again sees the bottle of
alcohol she recommences to cry, knowing what is in
store for her. Two days later, same reaction, as soon
as she sees the bottle and even before it is opened.
(Ibid., pp. 248–49)

Such behavior clearly demonstrates anticipation or
prevision on the part of the child. An action is anticipated
that is independent of the action in progress. During preceding periods actions of the child were *always* dependent
on the immediate actions in the environment. Jacqueline

would cry *when* alcohol was put on a cut, not *before* it was put on.

Object Concept

An important construction during this period is the concept of the constancies of shape and size of objects. Piaget and Inhelder comment:

> In fact, the *constancy of shapes* results from their sensori-motor construction at the time of the coordination of perspectives. During the first period (0-4 mos.) . . . when objects change their perspective such alterations are perceived (by the child) not as changes in the point of view of the subject relative to the object, but as actual transformations of the objects themselves. The baby waggling his head before a hanging object behaves as if he acted upon it by jerking about, and it is not until the age of about 8–9 months that he really explores the perspective effects of actual displacements. Now it is just about this age (8–9 mos.) that he is first able . . . to reverse a feeding bottle presented to him wrong way round. That is, to attribute a fixed shape to a permanent solid.
>
> As for *size constancy* it is linked with the coordination of perceptually controlled movements. All through the first period (0–4 mos.) the child makes no distinction between movements of the object and those of his body. In the course of the second period (Stage 3 and 4) the subject begins to distinguish his own movements from those of the object. Here is found the beginning . . . of searching for objects when they disappear. It is in terms of this grouping of movements, and the permanence attributed to the object, that the latter acquires fixed dimensions and its size is estimated more or less correctly, regardless of whether it is near or distant. (Piaget and Inhelder 1956, p. 11)

As with other concepts, those of size and constancy develop in the expected manner. To the four-month-old child, different perspectives on objects appear to change the shape and size of the objects. Not until Period 4 are shape and size of objects stabilized concepts for the child.

During Period 4, a new dimension in the object concept of the child appears. Until this time, if an object the child has been playing with, such as a rattle, is placed under a blanket while the child is looking on, the child does not search after it. If an object is out of sight, it appears to no longer exist. Between the ages of 8 and 10 months (approximately), the child begins to search for objects that disappear, indicating that the child is aware the objects exist even when they cannot be seen. The rattle hidden under the blanket is retrieved. The following illustrates this new awareness of object permanence and some of its limitations:

> Observation 40.—At 0;10(18) Jacqueline is seated on a mattress without anything to disturb or distract her (no coverlets, etc.). I take her parrot from her hands and hide it twice in succession under the mattress, on her left, in *A*. Both times Jacqueline looks for the object immediately and grabs it. Then I take it from her hands and move it very slowly before her eyes to the corresponding place on her right, under the mattress, in *B* (sequential displacement). Jacqueline watches this movement very attentively, but at the moment when the parrot disappears in *B*, she turns to her left and looks where it was before, in *A*.
>
> During the next four attempts I hide the parrot in *B* every time without having first placed it in *A*. Each time Jacqueline watches me attentively. Nevertheless each time she immediately tries to rediscover the object in *A*; she turns the mattress over and examines it conscientiously. (Piaget 1954, p. 51)

Clearly, Jacqueline searches for objects that disappear. To do this she must have a concept that objects still exist after they disappear from view. But her searches are limited; she searches for objects only where they usually disappear, not always where they are viewed to disappear.

Concept of Causality

During Period 4, the child for the first time shows awareness that objects (besides himself) can cause activity. Until this time, the child typically considered his own actions as the cause of all things. The following illustrates this change in the concept of causality:

> 0;8(7) [Laurent]. . . . A moment later I lower my hand very slowly, starting very high up and directing it toward his feet, finally tickling him for a moment. He bursts out laughing. When I stop midway, he grasps my hand or arm and pushes it toward his feet.
> At 0;9(0) he grasps my hand and places it against his belly which I have just tickled.
> At 0;9(13) Laurent is in his baby swing which I shake three or four times by pulling a cord; he grasps my hand and presses it against the cord. (Ibid., p. 26)

Piaget commented:

> . . . the cause of a certain phenomenon is no longer identified by the child with the feeling he has of acting upon this phenomenon. The subject begins to discover that a spatial contact exists between cause and effect and so any object at all can be a source of activity (and not only his own body). (Piaget 1952c, p. 212)

For the first time, there is an elementary externalization of causality. The child is aware that objects other than the self can be the causes of actions.

Affect

During the second year of life, three affective developments are noteworthy. The first is that feelings begin to play a role in determining means used to achieve goals as well as determining goals. Things that are useful in attaining goals come to take on value to the child.

Second, children begin to experience "success" and "failure" from an affective point of view. Feelings associated with particular actions or activities are preserved (remembered). Children are attracted to activities at which they are successful.

In learning to walk, for example, previous success or failure can be seen to influence the interest and endeavor. This clearly indicates that some sort of self-estimation is taking place. (Piaget 1981, p. 32)

Third, in Periods 5 and 6, children begin to invest affectivity in (transfer affect to) others. Until this time, feelings have revolved around the self. With the cognitive differentiation of the self from other objects (object concept), feelings such as liking and disliking can begin to be directed toward others as objects. The investment of affect in others is the first clear "social" development.

PERIOD 5 (12-18 MONTHS)

In previous periods a child developed coordination between schemata for vision and touch that permitted him or her to prolong unusual events (Period 3) and subsequently become able to coordinate familiar schemata in solving *new* problems (Period 4). In Period 5 the child attains a higher level of operation when he or she begins to form *new* schemata to solve new problems. The child develops *new* means to ends through "experimentation" rather than through the application of habitual, previously formed schemata. In this case, both *new* schemata and *new* coordinations are present. When confronted with a problem not solvable by the use of available schemata, the child can be seen to experiment, and through a trial-and-error process, to develop *new* means (schemata). This appears in several examples:

Observation 167.—At 1;3(12) Jacqueline throws a plush dog outside the bars of her playpen and she tries to catch it. Not succeeding, she then pushes the pen itself in the right direction! By holding onto the frame with one hand while with the other she tried to grasp the dog, she observed that the frame was mobile. She had accordingly, without wishing to do so, moved it away from the dog. She at once tried to correct this movement and thus saw the pen approach its objective. These two fortuitous discoveries then led her to utilize movements of the playpen and to push it at first experimentally, then systematically. There was a moment's groping, but it was short.

    At 1;3(16), on the other hand, Jacqueline right away pushes her playpen in the direction of the objects to be picked up. (Piaget 1952, p. 315)

In the example, Jacqueline "experiments" with playpen moving. The utility of this behavior evolves after much trial-and-error experimentation. With experience, a *new* schema is developed (playpen moving) and results in the solution of a problem previously unsolvable to the child.

In the first half of the second year, the child spends much time "experimenting" with objects, as in the example above. In the bathtub, objects are repeatedly pushed under water; things are splashed. The child typically is very intent on seeing how objects behave in *new* situations. For the first time, the child is able to adapt (accommodate) to unfamiliar situations by finding new means.

In terms of intellectual development, these new behaviors are particularly important. Piaget suggested that behavior becomes intelligent when the child acquires the ability to solve new problems.

    . . . it can be said that the mechanism of empirical intelligence has been definitely formed. The child is henceforth capable of resolving new problems, even if no acquired (currently available) schema is directly utilizable for this purpose, and if the solution of these problems has not yet been found by deduction or representation, it is insured in principle in all cases due to the combined working of experimental search and the coordination of schemata. (Ibid., p. 265)

The child has reached a significant period in cognitive development when he or she becomes able to solve new sensori-motor problems. It marks the beginning of truly intelligent behavior, the development of which started when reflex activities began in the young infant.

Object Concept

As we have seen, around age 12 months, a child's behavior indicates an awareness that objects continue to exist even though they cannot be seen. Prior to Period 4, the child did not search for objects that were hidden, even though he or she viewed the disappearance. The rattle hidden under the blanket was not retrieved. In Period 4 (8–12 months) the child searches for objects that are hidden, but not always in the place where they are seen to be hidden. In this case, the child was said to be unable to handle *sequential displacements*; that is, if the rattle that is usually hidden in place *A* now is hidden in place *B*, the child searches for it in place *A*. In Period 5, the child typically accounts for sequential displacements; he or she searches for objects in the position resulting from the last visible displacement, not in a special place. When the rattle is hidden in *A*, it is searched for in *A*; when it is hidden in *B*, it is searched for in *B*.

Still, the object concept is not yet fully developed. The child during Period 5 typically is able to follow displacements if they are visible, but remains unable to follow *invisible displacements*. The following illustrates this case:

> Observation 56.— . . . at 1;6(9), I resume the experiment but with a celluloid fish containing a rattle. I put the fish in the box under the rug. There I shake it and Jacqueline hears the fish in the box. I turn the box upside down and bring it out empty. Jacqueline immediately takes possession of the box, searches for the fish, turns the box over in all directions, looks around her, in particular looks at the rug but does not raise it.

> The next attempts yield nothing further. . . .
> That evening I repeat the experiment with a lit-
> tle lamb. Jacqueline herself puts the lamb in the box
> and when the whole thing is under the coverlet she
> says with me, "Coucou, lamb." When I take out the
> empty box she says, "Lamb, Lamb," but does not
> look under the coverlet.
> Whenever I leave the whole thing under the cov-
> erlet she immediately searches for the box and
> brings out the lamb. But when I start again, using
> the first technique, she no longer looks under the
> coverlet! (Piaget 1954, p. 69)

While the abilities developed during Period 5 permit
Jacqueline to solve problems involving sequential displacements, she cannot yet solve those involving invisible displacements. This ability will not come about until she
develops mental representation of objects (Period 6).

Concept of Causality

In the previous period the typical child demonstrates
an awareness that other objects beyond the self can be a
source of actions (causality). The following illustrates the
elaboration of the concept of causality in Period 5:

> At 1;3(30) Jacqueline holds in her right hand a
> box she cannot open. She holds it out to her mother,
> who pretends not to notice. Then she transfers the
> box from her right hand to her left, with her free
> hand grasps her mother's hand, opens it, and puts
> the box in it. The whole thing has occurred without a
> sound. . . .
> So also, during the next days, Jacqueline makes
> the adult intervene in the particulars of her game,
> whenever an object is too remote, etc.: she calls,
> cries, points to objects with her fingers, etc. In short,
> she well knows that she depends on the adult for sat-
> isfaction; the person of someone else becomes her
> best procedure for realization. (Ibid., p. 275)

Not only does Jacqueline demonstrate an awareness that other people can effect activity, but also that other objects can. The following illustration shows this clearly:

> Observation 175.—At 1;2(30) Jacqueline is standing in a room which is not hers and examines the green wallpaper. Then she touches it gently and at once looks at her fingertips. This is evidently the generalization of schemata . . . touching food (jams, etc.) and looking at her fingers. . . .
>
> At 1;3(12) she is standing in her playpen and I place a clown, which she recently received, on the top of the frame, in different places in sequence. Jacqueline advances laboriously along the frame but, when she arrives in front of the clown, she grasps it very cautiously and delicately, knowing that it will fall at the slightest shake. She behaved in this way ever since the first attempt. . . . Jacqueline foresees certain properties of the object which are independent of its action with respect to herself. The green wallpaper is conceived as though it ought to leave colored traces, . . . and the clown as falling down at the first touch. (Piaget 1952c, pp. 327–28)

In these examples, Jacqueline clearly sees objects (wallpaper, clown) as the causes of possible phenomena that are external to her actions. Prevision is seen that is *not* based on sequences of actions already observed in the same form (the wallpaper and doll are new to Jacqueline). Thus objects beyond the self are for the first time seen as causes of actions.

PERIOD 6 (18–24 MONTHS)

During Period 6, a child moves from the sensori-motor level of intelligence to representational intelligence. That is, the child becomes able to internally (mentally) represent objects and events and subsequently becomes able to solve problems through representation (cognitively). In Period 5, new means for solutions to problems were attained through active experimentation. In Period 6, the child develops new means also, but there is no reliance on experimentation as in the previous stage. For the first time, invention of means is arrived at by trying out action sequences at the representational level in the head (thinking) rather than in active experimentation. In effect, the experimentation is done in thought (through representation of actions) rather than through movement or actions. The following illustrates Period 6 invention of means, through representation and mental activity:

> Observation 181.—At 1;6(23) for the first time Lucienne plays with a doll carriage whose handle comes to the height of her face. She rolls it over the carpet by pushing it. When she comes against a wall, she pulls, walking backward. But as this position is not convenient for her, she pauses and without hesitation, goes to the other side to push the carriage again. She therefore found the procedure in one attempt, apparently through analogy to other situations but without training, apprenticeship, or chance.
>
> In the same kind of inventions, that is to say, in the realm of kinematic[4] representation, the following fact should be cited. At 1;10(27) Lucienne tries to kneel before a stool, but, by leaning against it, pushes it further away. She then raises herself up, takes it and places it against a sofa. When it is firmly set there she leans against it and kneels without difficulty. (Ibid., p. 338)

Lucienne, in these examples, demonstrates the sudden invention of a solution to sensori-motor problems along with an awareness of causality. This kind of invention and the lack of overt experimentation suggests that the solutions are arrived at internally through mental combinations, independent of immediate experiences.

> . . . instead of being controlled at each of these stages and *a posteriori* by the facts themselves, the searching is controlled *a priori* by mental combination. Before trying them, the child foresees which

maneuvers will fail and which will succeed. . . .
Moreover, the procedure conceived as being capable
of succeeding is in itself new, that is to say, it results
from an original mental combination and not from a
combination of movements actually executed at each
stage of the operation. (Ibid., pp. 340–41)

Thus a child becomes able to construct possible solutions to problems mentally by carrying out possible action sequences in his or her head (in representations). For about two years this ability has been gradually evolving from sensori-motor behaviors. At this stage the child can arrive at solutions to simple motor problems without the aid of sensori-motor experimentation or the assistance of concurrent experiences.

Object Concept

The ability of the Period 6 child to internally represent events is reflected in the child's object concept. Representation allows the child to find objects that are hidden by invisible displacement. That is, the child cannot only find objects when they are visibly hidden, but representation of possibilities permits the child to search for, and find, objects that he or she does not see hidden. This amounts to a measure of liberation from immediate perceptions. The child knows objects are permanent. The following observation of Jacqueline demonstrates this awareness:

Observation 64.—At 1;7(20) Jacqueline watches
me when I put a coin in my hand, then put my hand
under a coverlet. I withdraw my hand closed; Jacqueline opens it, then searches under the coverlet
until she finds the object. I take back the coin at
once, put it in my hand and then slip my closed hand
under a cushion situated at the other side (on her left
and no longer on her right); Jacqueline immediately
searches for the object under the cushion. I repeat
the experiment by hiding the coin under a jacket;
Jacqueline finds it without hesitation.

II. I complicate the test as follows: I place the coin in my hand, then my hand under the cushion. I bring it forth closed and immediately hide it under the coverlet. Finally I withdraw it and hold it out, closed, to Jacqueline. Jacqueline then pushes my hand aside without opening it (she guesses that there is nothing in it, which is new), she looks under the cushion, then directly under the coverlet where she finds the object. . . .

I then try a series of three displacements: I put the coin in my hand and move my closed hand sequentially from A to B and from B to C; Jacqueline sets my hand aside, then searches in A, in B and finally in C.

Lucienne is successful in the same tests at 1;3(14). (Piaget 1954, p. 79)

The ability of the child to maintain "images" of objects (representation) when they are absent is clearly seen in the above example. The displacement of objects results in a search on the child's part until they are found.

Concept of Causality

As with the object concept and other development, a child's awareness of causality is greatly enhanced by his or her new ability to internally represent objects. Through Period 5, the child remains unable to predict true cause-effect relationships in his or her sensori-motor world.

Just as during the sensorimotor development of objects and the spatial field the child becomes capable of evoking absent objects and of representing to himself displacements not given as such in the perceptual field, so also at the sixth stage the child become capable of reconstructing causes in the presence of their effects alone, and without having perceived the action of those causes. Inversely, given a certain perceived object as the source of potential actions, he becomes capable of foreseeing and representing to himself its future effects. (Ibid., p. 293)

The following example demonstrates Laurent's concept of causality at this stage. Clearly through representation, he accurately predicts a cause-and-effect relationship.

> At 1;4(4) . . . Laurent tries to open a garden gate but cannot push it forward because it is held back by a piece of furniture. He cannot account either visually or by any sound for the cause that prevents the gate from opening, but after having tried to force it he suddenly seems to understand; he goes around the wall, arrives at the other side of the gate, moves the armchair which holds it firm, and opens it with a triumphant expression. (Ibid., p. 296)

Again, the rapid invention of solutions to problems is seen. Such solutions were not seen in behaviors prior to Period 6. From Laurent's actions, we can infer representation of objects, a clear object concept, and a clear understanding of causality in a sensori-motor problem.

> In a general way, therefore, at the sixth stage the child is now capable of causal deduction and is no longer restricted to perception of sensorimotor utilization of the relations of cause to effect. (Ibid., p. 297)

Affect

By the end of the sensori-motor period, young children have typically developed affective feelings and preferences that are distinct from their earlier reflexive responses. Reflexes continue to operate, but behavior is now directed in part by new affective (and cognitive) capabilities. Feelings become factors in deciding what to do and what not to do. Thus the affective world of the two-year-old is very different from that of the newborn.

The cognitive differentiation of the self as an object and others as objects opens the door for true social interchange. Young children become capable of investing affect in (having feelings for) other people. Likes and dislikes for

others are established, and initial interpersonal relationships begin to form. With the child's affective and cognitive
capabilities expanded through continuous construction,
relationships with others

> . . . start to become true exchange relationships
> between the self and the other person. These ex-
> changes make more important, more structured,
> and more stable valuations possible. Such valuations
> indicate the beginning of interpersonal "moral feel-
> ings." (Piaget 1981, p. 41)

Moral Development

Early in his career Piaget became interested in children's concepts of rules and other moral feelings. His major
work in this area was *The Moral Judgment of the Child* (1965),
originally published in 1932. Piaget studied the development of children's concepts of game rules. Marbles was one
game studied because it has a rule structure and was a
favorite game of children at that time.

Piaget discovered, as we see in later chapters, that
children's understanding of rules and other moral concepts
(cheating, lying, justice, to name a few) develops in a manner essentially the same as cognitive concepts and other
affective concepts. Moral concepts are constructed.

As one might suspect, there is no evidence of understanding game rules or other moral concepts during the
sensori-motor period. During the first few years of life, which
frequently extend into the preoperational period (years
2–7) of cognitive development, activity games such as marbles are played according to the whim of the child. Children
at this level do not understand rules at all. The activity is
nonsocial. To the sensori-motor child, marbles are simply
objects to be explored and little else, with the child's enjoyment coming from this activity.

While children at two years of age typically have not
yet started to construct moral concepts, they clearly have

developed affective feelings, preferences, and likes and dislikes; and they are entering the social realm. These experiences are necessary for the development of moral feelings and further affective development in general. From this point onward, the child's world becomes increasingly influenced by interactions with others.

SUMMARY

The child at age 2 is cognitively different from the infant at birth. This chapter has presented Piaget's conceptualization of how this transformation takes place. At birth, the child's behavior is reflexive. Toward the second month of life, an infant makes primitive differentiations of objects in his or her immediate environment, primarily via the sucking reflex. Between the fourth and eighth months, coordination of vision and touch typically occurs for the first time. The child grasps what it sees (Period 3). Toward the end of the first year, the child begins to develop object permanence and awareness that objects other than himself or herself can cause events. Two (or more) familiar schemata are coordinated to solve new problems (Period 4). Early in the second year, true intelligent behavior typically evolves; the child constructs *new* means to solving problems through "experimentation." Also the child sees himself or herself as an object among objects (Period 5). Toward the end of the second year, the child becomes able to internally represent objects and events. This ability liberates the child from sensori-motor intelligence, permitting the invention of *new* means to solve problems through mental activity.

Do infants construct knowledge? In Piaget's view they clearly do. The functioning of assimilation and accommodation are evident shortly after birth. Much of the knowledge constructed during the first two years of life is *physical knowledge*, knowledge about the physical characteristics of objects. An infant discovers properties of objects in his or her environment by manipulating them. Most of the discussion in this chapter has been directed at the child's development of *logical-mathematical knowledge*. Concepts about causality, space, and the object concept are examples of logical-mathematical concepts. Each deals with relationships and is created mentally by the child.

Concurrent with the development of cognitive structures is the development of affective structures. We have seen that at birth an infant's reactions are primarily reflexive (as in crying) and lack differentiation. With initial cognitive differentiations, the first acquired feelings are observed. These are connected with the infant's actions. In the second year of life, likes and dislikes are observed, and affect begins to play a role in the selection and avoidance of actions. Throughout most of the first two years of life, affect is invested in the self and in one's own activities, largely because the young infant has not cognitively constructed the notion that the world is composed of many physically independent objects of which the infant (the self) is one. As a result, during the second year of life comes the possibility of investing affect in objects other than the self (in other people). This is when likes and dislikes of others are first expressed.

An infant is born asocial. At the outset nothing he or she does involves true social interchange. By the end of the second year of life, the typical infant is developmentally at the point where true social interchanges become possible.

The cognitive development of the sensori-motor stage evolves as a child acts on the environment. The child's actions are *spontaneous*. The motivation for particular actions is internal. The adapting and organizing of assimilation and accommodation operate from the beginning, resulting in the continuous qualitative and quantitative change in schemata. The child can be seen as constructing knowledge at a primitive level, trying to make sense of the surrounding world.

Each new period is characterized by behaviors reflecting qualitatively superior cognitive structures. In the development of intelligence during the first two years of life, it can be seen that each new period of development incorporates previous periods. The new periods do not displace the

TYPICAL SERIATION CONSTRUCTIONS AT DIFFERENT
AGE LEVELS

old, but improve upon them. In the same way, each stage
of development helps to explain stages that follow. So it is
throughout the course of cognitive development.

As the infant develops cognitively, the changes pro-
moted affect behavior in all areas. Concepts do not develop
independent of one another. For example, in Period 4 (8-12
months), the typical child becomes able for the first time
to systematically turn a bottle around so that he or she can
get the nipple. What does this imply about the child's concepts or schemata? First, the behavior suggests the child is
aware of the constancy of shape of objects. Objects do not
change in shape when perspectives on them change (object
concept). Since all actions occur in space, the child must
also have a functional concept of space and the relationships between objects. Also, the behavior of turning the bottle around is clearly an *intentional* act requiring a measure
of hand-eye *coordination*. Each of these abilities evolves at
about the same time. Their paths of development are one.
As a child assimilates and accommodates, all his or her

schemata are elaborated. Thus it is that evolving behaviors reflect qualitative changes in many schemata.

Upon completing the development of the sensori-motor stage (it can be before or after age 2), the child has reached a point of conceptual development that is necessary for the development of spoken language and other cognitive and social skills during the next major stage in cognitive development: the preoperational stage. From this point on, the child's intellectual development takes place increasingly in the conceptual-symbolic area rather than exclusively in the sensori-motor area. This does not imply that sensori-motor development ends; it means only that intellectual development is to be affected by representational, symbolic, and social activity rather than motor activity alone.

NOTES

1. Egocentrism is one of Piaget's most important concepts. In general it refers to the cognitive state in which the individual sees the world only from his or her point of view, without being aware that other points of view exist. Thus it is a state that the egocentric cannot be aware of. For the infant, egocentrism means an absence of self-perception, of the self as an object in a world of objects. This is only overcome when the infant's concept of object develops and subsequently permits the development of self-perception.

2. 0;1(4). Designations such as this refer to the age of the child at the time of the observation, with years, months, and days being referred to in that order. Laurent was 1 month, 4 days old at the time of observation.

3. Piaget used the term "circular reactions" to describe the young child's attempts to repeat interesting events. The repetition of events is felt to be important for several reasons. It is clearly an active attempt to assimilate experience. Circular reactions lead to a greater awareness of objects as objects, and lead to a greater understanding of cause and effect. Three kinds of circular reactions are described by Piaget (1967, 1969). *Primary circular reactions*, appearing in sensori-motor Period 2, involve actions that involve only the infant's body, such as moving a hand from side to side. *Secondary circular reactions* arise in Period 3 and are actions involving objects beyond the infant, such as repeatedly hitting the

side of the crib with an object. *Tertiary circular reactions* arise in Period 4 and are characterized by intentional variations in the repetitions to see what effects similar actions have. The infant might, for example, hit different parts of the crib with an object.

4. The science of motions considered apart from their causes and as applied to mechanical contrivances.

Chapter 4

THE STAGE OF PREOPERATIONAL THOUGHT

During the preoperational stage (age 2–7 years), a child evolves from one who functions primarily in a sensori-motor mode and whose "thinking" is through actions into one who functions increasingly in a conceptual and representational mode. The child becomes increasingly able to internally represent events (think) and becomes less dependent on his or her current sensori-motor actions for direction of behavior.

Between the ages of 2 and 7, the child's thought is characterized by newly emerging abilities. Several of the most important characteristics of preoperational thought are discussed in this chapter. The development of representational skills and the socialization of behavior are presented first. These are followed by a discussion of characteristics of thought of the preoperational child. These characteristics are egocentrism, centration, a lack of reversibility, and the inability to follow transformations.

REPRESENTATION

The major development during the preoperational stage is the ability to represent objects and events. Several kinds of representation have significance in development. In order of their emergence they are *deferred imitation*, *symbolic play*, *drawing*, *mental imagery*, and *spoken language*. Each kind of representation begins to emerge around age 2. Each is a form of representation in the sense that something other than objects and events (a signifier) is used to represent objects and events (the signified). Piaget referred to this as the *symbolic function*, or the *semiotic function*, the use of symbols or signs.

Symbols are things that bear some resemblance to what they represent: drawings, silhouettes, and so forth. Signs are arbitrary things that bear no resemblance to what they represent. Written and spoken language and numbers are examples of systems of signs.

Let us consider each of the five forms of representation mentioned above.

Deferred Imitation

As early as the third month of an infant's life, attempts to imitate others who are present can be observed. It is not until the second year of life that the first true forms of mental representation occur. Deferred imitation is the imitation of objects and events that have not been present for some time. For example, the child who plays patty-cake by himself, imitating an earlier session with his parents, is engaging in deferred imitation. The significance of deferred imitation is that it implies that the child has developed the ability to mentally represent (remember) the behavior imitated. Without representation, deferred imitation would be impossible. Because the child usually tries to accurately copy a prior behavior, imitation is primarily an accommodation.

Symbolic Play

The second form of representation that preoperational children engage in is symbolic play. One might observe a child with a block of wood, playing with it as if it were a car and giving it all the attributes of a car. This is symbolic play, a game of pretending, a kind of activity not found in the sensori-motor stage (Wadsworth 1978).

The nature of symbolic play is that it is imitative, but it is also a form of self-expression with only the self as the intended audience. There is no intention of communicating with others. In symbolic play the child, without constraints, constructs symbols (which may be unique), inventions that represent anything he or she wishes. There is an assimilation of reality to the self rather than an accommodation of the self to reality (as in deferred imitation). As Piaget wrote in 1967: "Its [symbolic play] function is to satisfy the self by transforming what is real into what is desired" (p. 23).

The child's intended meaning in play may or may not be apparent to the viewer. Because there is no accommodating focus in symbolic play, as there is in imitation and drawing, and because symbolic play is not directed at an audience other than the self, what the child is representing in play is frequently totally unclear to the observer. While we may recognize the child's play with a block as pretending it to be a car, we may not recognize the child curled up motionless on the floor as pretending to be a sleeping animal.

Children's play may, on the surface, appear to be of little value to the cognitive and affective development of the child. Yet Piaget assures us that the free ranging nature of symbolic play has an essentially functional value and is not simply a diversion.

> In symbolic play this systematic assimilation takes the form of a particular use of the semiotic (symbolic) function—namely, the creation of symbols at will in order to express everything in the child's life experience that cannot be formulated and assimilated by means of language alone. (Piaget and Inhelder 1969, p. 61)

Thus, when language is not sufficiently available or is inappropriate in the child's view, symbolic play is a forum for ideas, thoughts, and concerns.

Drawing

The early preoperational child's use of crayon, pencil, and brush initially amounts to scribbling. At first there is no preconception on the child's part of drawing (representing) something, though sometimes forms emerge during the course of scribbling. Over the course of the preoperational stage, children increasingly attempt to represent things through drawings, and their efforts become more realistic.

Young children's drawings are usually realistic in intent, though the drawings are confounded by the fact that up until eight or nine years of age children draw what they think rather than what they see—what is visually accurate. Thus, if five- or six-year-olds are asked to draw a house and trees on the side of a hill, they draw them perpendicular to the side of the hill. Not until age 8 or 9 or so are they able to coordinate the hill and the plane of the earth and draw objects perpendicular to the earth.

Mental Images

Mental images are internal representations (symbols) of objects and past perceptual experiences, although they are not accurate copies of those experiences. Images *are not* copies of perceptions stored in the mind. As drawings bear

FIGURE 4.1

a resemblance to what they represent, so too mental images are *imitations* of perceptions and necessarily bear a similarity to the perceptions themselves. In this sense, images are thought to be symbols.

There is no evidence of the existence of images in the mind of the sensori-motor child. During the preoperational stage, images are primarily static. According to Piaget and Inhelder (1969), images of movements begin to appear at the concrete operational level. Thus mental images during this stage are more like drawings or photographs (static) than they are like movies.

Spoken Language

The single most evident development during the preoperational stage is the development of spoken language, the last form of representation to be discussed. Around two years of age (give or take a few months), the typical child begins to use spoken words as symbols in place of objects. A sound (word) comes to represent an object. Initially the child uses "one-word" sentences, but his or her language facility expands quickly. By age 4 the typical child has largely mastered the use of spoken language. The child can speak and use most grammatical rules, and can understand what is heard if it contains familiar vocabulary. Children prior to this stage of development may use words. They may say "mama" or "dada" during the first year. These early words are usually not used to *represent* objects and are not language in the representational sense.

The rapid development of this form of symbolic representation (spoken language) is instrumental in facilitating the rapid conceptual development that takes place during this stage. Regarding the effects of language on intellectual life, Piaget wrote:

> This [language] has three consequences essential to mental development: (1) the possibility of verbal exchange with other persons, which heralds the onset of the socialization of action; (2) the internalization of words, i.e., the appearance of thought itself, supported by internal language and a system of

signs; (3) last and most important, the internalization of action of such which from now on, rather than being purely perceptual and motor as it has been heretofore, can represent itself intuitively by means of pictures and "mental experiments." (Piaget 1967, p. 17)

THE DEVELOPMENT OF SPOKEN LANGUAGE

Spoken language (and other forms of representation)[1] opens doors to the child that were not open before. The internalization of behavior through representation, facilitated by language, acts to "speed up" the rate at which experience can take place. During the sensori-motor stage, "experience" took place only as rapidly as movement could occur. The child, in effect, had to carry out actions in order to "think." (Movement produced "thought.") With the development of representation during the preoperational stage, thinking can occur in part through representations of actions rather than actions alone. Representational thought is carried out more rapidly than thought through movement because the former is not tied to direct experience.

In 1926 Piaget suggested, on the basis of his observations of young children's conversations, that there are essentially two classifications of the preoperational child's speech: (1) egocentric speech, and (2) socialized speech. Egocentric speech is characterized by a lack of real communication; socialized speech is characterized by communication. From age 2 to age 4 or 5, a child's speech is in part lacking in communicative intent. The child speaks in the presence of others, but without any apparent intention that others should hear his words. Even though the child speaks with others, there is no communication. Nonconversations of this type Piaget called *collective monologues*. Such speech is clearly egocentric. The following example demonstrates the noncomunicative egocentric speech of the early preoperational child:

> Mlle. L. tells a group of children that owls cannot see by day.

Lev: "Well, I know quite well that it can't."

Lev (at a table where a group is at work): "I've already done moons so I'll have to change it."

Lev (picks up some barley sugar crumbs): "I say, I've got a lovely pile of eye-glasses."

Lev: "I say, I've got a gun to kill him with. I say, I am the captain on horseback. I say, I've got a horse and a gun as well." (Ibid., p. 41)

These examples of speech are clearly egocentric. Lev is simply thinking out his actions aloud, with no desire to give anyone any information. He is having a conversation with himself in the presence of others (collective monologue).

By age 6 or 7, language has become intercommunicative. Children's conversations clearly involve an exchange of ideas. In the following, Lev, now considerably older than in the previous example, communicates with others in his conversations:

Pie (6;5): "Now, you shan't have it [the pencil] because you asked for it.—" Hei (6;0): "Yes I will, because it's mine.—" Pie: "Course it isn't yours. It belongs to everybody, to all the children." —Lev (6;0): "Yes, it belongs to Mlle. L. and all the children. . . ." Pie: "It belongs to Mlle. L. because she bought it, and it belongs to all the children as well." (Ibid., p. 88)

Clearly the above illustration involves communication. Lev in the earlier example spoke only to himself. Here he speaks to others and clearly intends them to hear.

The development of language during the preoperational stage is seen by Piaget as a gradual transition from egocentric speech characterized by *collective monologue* to socialized intercommunicative speech.

How Children Learn Spoken Language

Spoken language is a form of social-arbitrary knowledge. The symbols used in a language bear no relationship to what they represent. Most children in all cultures begin to master their native language around age 2. Because language learning is so universal, one is tempted to believe that acquisition of spoken language is automatic or innate. Piaget's theory suggests that this is not the case and that spoken language is acquired (learned).

Certainly one of the most difficult and complex tasks we face in our lives, considering the level of development when it occurs, is learning to use and understand spoken language. At two years of age children begin to master spoken language, a system of arbitrary signs.[2] Children receive no formal instruction in learning spoken language, though models are usually present. By and large, children master the use of the language fairly quickly. Is there a learning task of equivalent difficulty with which adults at an advanced level of development are confronted? I think not.

Piaget's theory suggests that the motivation for learning spoken language is the *adaptation value* of doing so. The child who learns one word as representation (such as "drink" or "cookie") thus is able to more effectively communicate with his or her caretakers and have personal needs met. Thus, language learning has immediate and long-lasting value (adaptation value) to the child.[3]

How do children learn spoken language? Children acquire spoken language the same way they acquire all other knowledge. The child constructs the language. At the outset, the child's task is similar to code breaking. The child figures out (constructs) the rules of the language from his or her experience.[4] With experience, children's constructions become refined (the code is more thoroughly broken). Much progress is made between age 2 and age 4.

LANGUAGE AND THOUGHT

The relationship between language and thought is an important one. Piaget's formulation of sensori-motor development demonstrates that the rudiments of intelligent behavior evolve *before* language develops.

> Intelligence actually appears well before lan-
> guage, that is to say, well before internal thought,
> which presupposes the use of verbal signs (internal-
> ized language). It is an entirely practical intelligence
> based on the manipulation of objects; in place of
> words and concepts it uses precepts and movements
> organized into "action schema." For example, to
> grab a stick in order to draw up a remote object is an
> act of intelligence (and a fairly late developing one at
> that: about eighteen months). Here, an instrument,
> the means to an end, is coordinated with a pre-
> established goal. . . . Many other examples could
> be cited. (Piaget 1967, p. 11)

Piaget contended that the emergence of internal representation (of which spoken language is one form) increases
the powers of thought in range and speed. He suggested
that there are three major differences between representational and sensori-motor behavior: (1) The sequence of
events in sensori-motor patterns is restricted to the speed
of sensori-motor acts, making sensori-motor intelligence very
slow. On the other hand, verbal behavior permits the representation of many actions very quickly. (2) Sensori-motor
adaptations are limited to the immediate actions of the child,
while language permits thought and adaptation to range
beyond present activity. (3) Sensori-motor intelligence proceeds in a one-step-at-a-time fashion, while representational thought and language permit the child to simultaneously handle many elements in an organized manner
(Piaget and Inhelder 1969, p. 86).

Thus, because language is a form of representation of
objects and events, thought involving language is liberated
from the limitations of the direct action of sensori-motor
thought. Cognitive activity can proceed rapidly and with a
range and speed not previously available.

Another important question is whether language (in a
simplistic sense) determines logical thought or whether
thought determines language. Every language has a logical
structure that is a socially elaborated system for relationships, classifications, and so on. The language exists before

the child exists. Does this mean that the logic of language is the source of all the logic of the child, or does the child invent and create his or her own logic? In 1969 Piaget and Inhelder cited two kinds of studies that supported their contention that language is neither a necessary nor a sufficient condition to ensure the development of logical thought. Studies of deaf mutes (no spoken language) showed that they develop logical thought in the same sequential stages as normal children, but with a one- to two-year delay in some operations. This suggests that language is not necessary for the development of logical operations, though it clearly acts as a facilitator. Other studies of blind children, with normal verbal development, demonstrated longer delays, up to four years on the same tasks. Blind children are hindered from birth in the development of sensori-motor schemata, and normal verbal performance does not compensate for this.

For Piaget, the development of language is based on the prior development of sensori-motor operations. Thus the development of sensori-motor operations is necessary for language development and not the other way around. Only after achieving the capability to internally represent experience do (can) children begin to construct spoken language. When language develops, there is a parallel development of conceptual abilities that language helps to facilitate, probably because language and representation permit conceptual activity to proceed more rapidly than sensori-motor operations do. The development is seen as a facilitator of cognitive development (as in deaf children) but not as a prerequisite for it nor as necessary for it.

The development of physical and logical-mathematical knowledge rests on the activity of the child. Children construct knowledge out of spontaneous actions. Language does not play any direct role in the construction of physical and logical-mathematical knowledge. In the construction of social-arbitrary knowledge, the role of spoken language is primarily one of providing an efficient means of *communication* between the child and others. This helps to make social experience more accessible to the child.

THE SOCIALIZATION OF BEHAVIOR

Behavior is considered social when it involves clear interchanges between people. The process of socialization begins long before behavior is social. Socialization can be traced back to the latter part of the first year of life when a child first begins to imitate other people. The process of imitation (a form of accommodation) develops until the child shows deferred imitation (imitation of absent objects) around age 2. During the preoperational stage, socialization of the child's behavior can be seen in several activities including children's verbal exchanges and their play in games with rules (Piaget and Inhelder 1969, p. 119).

Our discussion of language pointed out that during the early part of the preoperational stage, children's use of spoken language is primarily composed of collective monologue conversations. Children usually speak in the presence of others as if they are speaking to themselves. They do not ask questions or exchange information most of the time. Verbal behavior is not very comunicative and not truly social. Not until age 6–7 does most of children's verbal behavior become clearly communicative and social.

Although Piaget primarily investigated cognitive or intellectual development, he indicated throughout his work his belief that all forms of development (cognitive, social, affective, and so on) evolve in an interrelated and parallel way. Intellectual and social developments do not evolve on separate schedules. Reasoning and knowledge impose constraints on the level of social reasoning that a child can develop.

CHARACTERISTICS OF PREOPERATIONAL THOUGHT

Piaget suggested that there are three levels of relationship between the actions of a child and his or her thought. The first is the sensori-motor level of direct action upon the environment. Between birth and age 2 all schemata are sensori-motor and dependent on the actions of the child. And the third, after age 7 or 8, is the level of operations, or logical thought. The child becomes able to reason in a way that is not dependent on immediate perceptual and motor actions (the stage of concrete operations). Between the ages 2 and 7 is the preoperational stage or prelogical period, which is an advance over sensori-motor intelligence but is not as advanced as the logical operations of later stages. Cognitive behavior is still influenced by perceptual activities. Actions are internalized via representational functions, but thought is still tied to perception (Piaget and Inhelder 1969, p. 93).

The following characteristics of preoperational thought are necessary for continuous development. In addition, they serve as obstacles to complete logical thought. The "obstacles" to logical thought presented are egocentrism, transformations, centration, and reversibility.

Egocentrism

Piaget characterized a preoperational child's behavior and thinking as *egocentric*. That is, the child cannot take the role of, or see the viewpoint of, another. He (or she) believes that everyone thinks the same way he does and that everyone thinks the same things he does. As a result, the child never questions his own thoughts because they are, as far as he is concerned, the only thoughts possible and consequently must be correct.

The preoperational child does not reflect on his own thoughts. As a result, he is never motivated to question his thinking, even when he is confronted with evidence that is contradictory to his thoughts. Where contradiction is present, the egocentric child concludes the evidence must be wrong because his thoughts are correct. Thus the child's thinking, from his point of view, is always logical and correct.

This egocentrism of thought is not egocentric by intent. The child remains unaware that he is egocentric and consequently never seeks to resolve it. Egocentrism is manifest in all the behavior of the preoperational child. As stated before, the two- to six-year-old's language and social behavior are largely egocentric. The child talks to himself when in the presence of others (in collective monologues) and frequently does not listen to others. Verbal behavior involves very little exchange of information and is nonsocial for the most part.

It is not until around age 6 or 7 that children's thoughts and those of their peers clearly conflict. Children begin to accommodate to others, and egocentric thought begins to give way to social pressure. Peer-group social interaction, the repeated conflict of one's own thoughts with those of others, eventually jars the child to question and seek verification of his thoughts. The very source of conflict, social interaction, becomes the child's source of verification. To be sure, verification of one's thoughts comes about only through comparison with the thoughts of others. Thus, peer-group social interaction is the primary factor that acts to dissolve cognitive egocentrism.

While egocentrism pervades the behavior of the preoperational child, it should not be thought that egocentric behavior does not occur in other stages of development. The sensori-motor child is totally egocentric at birth (in a sensori-motor sense: unable to differentiate himself from other objects), and continues to be so throughout most of the first two years of life. Indeed, egocentrism is a characteristic of thought that is *always* present during the initial attainment and use of any new cognitive structure (schema) or level of reasoning. Later we shall see that the adolescent, upon developing completely logical thought (formal operations), is very egocentric in the use of the newly acquired structures. Like other cognitive characteristics, egocentrism is not at a constant level throughout the stage. The child age 2–4 is much more consistently egocentric than the child age 6–7. As development proceeds, egocentrism slowly wanes and is revived in a different form when new cognitive structures are attained. Thus, egocentrism is a characteristic that pervades thought in some way in all periods of development.

Egocentric thinking, while a necessary characteristic of preoperational thought, in a sense acts to restrict the development of intellectual structures during the preoperational stage. Because the child is never required by his own reasoning to question his thinking or validate his concepts, intellectual development is restricted at that time. Egocentrism can be viewed as acting to inhibit disequilibrium. Egocentrism acts to maintain the structural status quo. Because the child does not question his own thinking, schemata are less likely to change through accommodation. While egocentrism in one sense limits cognitive development during the preoperational stage, it is an essential and natural part of the stage and of the initial use of any newly acquired cognitive characteristic.

Transformational Reasoning

Another characteristic of the preoperational child's thinking is his or her inability to reason successfully about transformations. While observing a sequence of changes or successive states, the child focuses exclusively on the *elements* in the sequence, or the successive states, rather than on the *transformation* by which one state is changed to another. The child does not focus on the process of transformation from an original state to a final state, but restricts his or her attention to each in between state when it occurs. The child moves from a particular perceptual event to a particular perceptual event, but cannot integrate a series of events in terms of any beginning-end relationships. Thought is neither inductive nor deductive; it is transductive.

For example, if a pencil is held upright as in Figure 4.2, and is allowed to fall, it passes from an original state (vertical) to a final state (horizontal) and through a series of successive states. Preoperational children, after viewing the pencil fall, typically cannot draw or otherwise reproduce the successive steps. They cannot attend to or reconstruct the transformation. They usually reproduce only the initial and final positions the pencil assumes.

A second example of the transformation problem is seen in a child walking through the woods. At different points along a trail the child sees snails—different snails each time. The child cannot tell whether they are all the same snail or

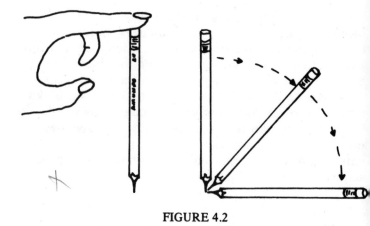

FIGURE 4.2

different snails. The child cannot reconstruct the *transformation* from event to event (snail to snail).

The inability of the preoperational child to follow transformations inhibits the development of logic in thought. Since the child is not aware of the relationship between events and all this can mean, comparisons between states of events are always incomplete.

Centration

Another characteristic of preoperational thought is what Piaget called *centration*. A child presented with a visual stimulus tends to center or fix attention on a limited perceptual aspect of the stimulus. The child seems unable to "explore" all aspects of the stimulus, or *de-center* the visual inspection. As a result the child, when centering, tends to assimilate only limited aspects of an event. Any cognitive activity seems to be dominated by the perceptual aspects. Perceptual evaluations dominate the cognitive evaluation (in the preoperational child), in much the same way as they did in the direct action of the sensori-motor child.

A child of age 4 or 5 who is asked to compare two rows of like objects in which one row contains 9 objects and the other, a longer row, contains only 7 objects (but spread farther apart) will typically select the perceptually longer row as having "more" objects. This will occur even when the child "knows" cognitively that 9 is more than 7. Perceptual evaluation will dominate cognitive evaluation.

The child tends to center on perceptual aspects of objects. It is only with time and experience that the child becomes able to *de-center* and evaluate perceptual events in a coordinated way with cognitions. After age 6 or 7, children reach the point where cognitions assume their proper position with respect to perceptions in thought.

Reversibility

According to Piaget, reversibility is the most clearly defined characteristic of intelligence (1963b, p. 41). If thought is reversible, it can follow the line of reasoning back to where it started. For example, a child without reversible thought is shown two equal-length rows of 8 coins each. She agrees that each has the same number of coins. One of the rows is lengthened while the child is watching. She no longer agrees that there are the same number of coins in each row. Part of her problem is that she is not able to mentally *reverse* the act of lengthening. She cannot maintain the equivalence of number in the face of perceptual change in a dimension that is irrelevant to number (length). Only when actions become reversible will she be able to solve such problems. The inability to reverse operations is seen in all the cognitive activity of the preoperational child.

Preoperational thought retains much of the rigidity of sensori-motor thought, although the preoperational surpasses it in quality. It is relatively inflexible, is dominated by perceptions, and is irreversible. The attainment of reversible operations is extremely difficult for a child. This is reasonable if one considers that *all* sensori-motor operations are irreversible by definition. Once a motor act is committed, it cannot be reversed. In much the same way, perceptions cannot be reversed. Thus representational acts, which are based on prior sensori-motor patterns and perceptions, must develop reversibility without any prior patterns to follow.

Sensori-motor and preoperational children construct concepts and knowledge about such things as space and causality from their actions on their environment. The environment contains physical elements and orderings; when these are acted on by the child, they permit concepts to be constructed or "discovered" (physical knowledge). Certain concepts or knowledge cannot be constructed or "discovered" directly from examples in the environment but must be invented by the child. This is true of many logical-mathematical concepts. For example, the environment does not contain many physical examples of reversibility a child can use as models for developing reversibility of thought and reasoning. Reversibility must therefore be invented by the child.

Piaget's concepts of egocentrism, centration, transformation, and reversibility are closely related. Early preoperational thought is dominated by the presence or absence of each of them. As cognitive development proceeds, these characteristics gradually subside in unison. A deterioration in egocentrism permits (requires) a child to de-center more and attend to simple transformations. All this in turn helps the child in the construction of reversibility.

CONSERVATION

The characteristics of preoperational thought described above can be viewed as obstacles to logical thought. Nonetheless, they are necessary for the development of logical thought—and they occur naturally. They are most clearly seen in what have come to be called conservation problems. The problems described in the pages that follow were developed by Piaget and his co-workers to assess children's levels of conceptual development and their level of attainment with respect to the concepts involved.

Conservation is the conceptualization that the amount or quantity of a matter stays the same regardless of any changes in an irrelevant dimension. For example, if we have a row of 8 pennies, and we move the pennies farther apart in the row, we still have 8 pennies. That is, the *number* of pennies does not change when a change is made in another, irrelevant dimension (in this case, the length of the row). An awareness of the number invariance would imply the ability to conserve number and that corresponding schemata have developed. Lack of this awareness implies a lack of number conservation and that corresponding schemata (reversibility) have not developed. This level of conservation ability is a measure of the kind of logical-mathematical structure a child has developed. During the preoperational stage, children typically cannot conserve; that is, they cannot hold one dimension invariant in the face of changes in other dimensions. By the end of the preoperational stage (age 7), some conservation structures are usually developed.

The development from nonconservation to conservation is a gradual one. As with all other changes in cognitive structures (schemata), the change is largely a function of the actions (cognitive and sensori-motor) of the child. According to Piaget, conservation structures cannot be induced through direct instruction (teaching) or reinforcement techniques. Active experience is the key. Conservation of number, area, and volume problems are presented next.

Conservation of Number

If a four- to five-year-old is presented with a row of checkers or other objects and asked to construct a row that is the same, he typically constructs a row of the same length, but his row may not correspond in the number of elements to the model. The typical construction proceeds by placing two checkers, one opposite each of the end checkers in the model, and then filling in a number of checkers without one-to-one correspondence. If there is correspondence, it is by accident (Piaget 1967, p. 31).

The typical five- to six-year-old is usually a little more systematic. When she is asked to perform the same conservation task, she uses one-to-one corespondence and makes each row equal in number and length to the model. But, if she sees one row lengthened (transformed as in Figure 4.3) without any change in the number of elements, she declares they are no longer equivalent. When asked for her *reasoning*, she typically indicates that one row has more because

FIGURE 4.3

it is longer. This is frequently true even if she counts the elements in each row. The preoperational child holds that the rows are equivalent only as long as there is visual correspondence in the length of arrays (ibid.).

The typical five- or six-year-old does not conserve number. He cannot see that the number of elements in a series does not change in the face of a perceptual change in a dimension irrelevant to number. According to Piagetian theory, what has happened is that after a transformation, the child makes a perceptual response instead of a cognitive response. This is inferred from the *reasoning* he provides for his answer.[5] In terms of previous notions of *centration*, the child focuses or centers on one aspect of the event—the length of the rows—and ignores another salient aspect of which he is cognitively aware: the number of objects. Also, the child does not focus on the *transformation* of stimulus arrays, but focuses on each successive state as if it were independent of the previous states. Thus the child, because of his inability to de-center and focus on the transformation, typically ends up making a perceptual response. Unable to *reverse* the changes he has seen occur, he resorts to a perceptual response. In this respect the child is "perception bound." When confronted with a problem where cognitive and perceptual solutions conflict, he makes decisions based on the perceptual cues.

Around the age of 6 or 7 the typical child learns to conserve number. Concurrently she *de-centers* her perceptions, attends to the *transformations*, and *reverses* operations. She constructs an awareness that a change in the length of a row of elements (an irrelevant dimension) does not change the number of elements in the row.

Conservation of Area

A second kind of conservation problem reflects a child's concept of *area*. This can be demonstrated by the cows-in-the-field problem (Piaget, Inhelder, and Szeminska 1960, p. 262). Two same-size sheets of green paper are placed before a child, and a toy or paper-cutout cow is placed in each field, as in Figure 4.4A. Several blocks of the same size are kept on hand to represent buildings. It is explained to the child that there are two fields of grass and a cow in each field. The child is asked, "Which cow has more grass to eat, or do they both have the same amount?" Typically, the response will be that both cows have the same amount of grass to eat. Once visual equivalence of area is established, the child is shown a barn (a block) being placed in each field, and the question is repeated: "Which cow has more grass to eat now, or do they both have the same amount?" Again, the response is typically that they both have the same amount of grass. A second block is placed in each field; but in the first field, the second block is placed away from

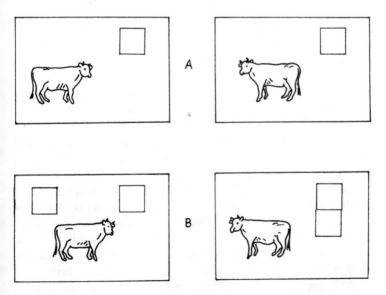

FIGURE 4.4

the first, and in the other field the second block is placed adjacent to the first (see Figure 4.4B). The question is repeated: "Which cow has more grass to eat now, or do they both have the same amount?" The child who cannot conserve typically says that the cow in the second field (blocks adjacent) has more grass to eat. The child's reasoning suggests that the field with two adjacent barns (one set of barns) has more grass area than the field with two separated barns (two sets of barns), even though the barns are seen as the same size. The child who can conserve says that they both have the same amount to eat. The conserver clearly reasons that the placement of barns is irrelevant to area. The important thing is the number of barns. The extension of this problem by more barn placements can be varied to check the reliability of conservation or nonconservation responses.[6]

Again, the nonconserving preoperational child has made a perceptual response. The second field looks like it has fewer buildings (because the buildings are attached) than the first field. The child is not able to de-center and attend to all salient aspects of the event, nor does he follow the *transformations* that have taken place. Each new placement is independent of the previous. Thus, as with conservation of number problems, the preoperational child fails to conserve. Not until age 7 to 8 is conservation of area with respect to this kind of problem usually attained.

Conservation of Liquid

A third kind of problem is the conservation of liquid volume problem. The preoperational child's inability to conserve liquid can usually be shown with the following task: A child is presented with two containers of equal size and shape, as in Figure 4.5. She is asked to compare the amount of liquid in the two containers. A few drops are added to one container, if necessary, to establish visual equivalence of volume. When equivalence is attained, the liquid from one of the glasses is poured into a taller and thinner glass (or shorter and wider glass), and the child is again asked to compare the two containers holding liquid.

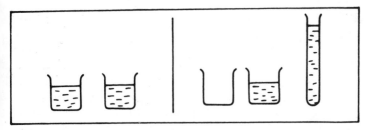

FIGURE 4.5

As in the previous problems, an irrelevant dimension (shape of the container) has been changed. The typical preoperational child does not see the two containers as equivalent in volume and declares that one or the other (usually the taller and thinner container) has more liquid. Reasoning is usually based on the height of one column of liquid compared with the height of the other. This is clearly a nonconservation response. If the liquid is then poured back into the original container, visual equivalence is usually achieved again for the child.

As in the previous conservation problems, the preoperational child typically does not attend to all aspects of *transformation* that she sees. She *centers* on the perceptual aspects of the problem. Because the column of water in the taller cylinder looks higher, it must contain more liquid. Reasoning is not logical. Reversibility is not present. It is not until the stage of concrete operations (age 7–11) that conservation of liquid volume is usually present.[7]

The preceding conservation problems illustrate but do not begin to exhaust the phenomenon of conservation. Qualitative differences in the logical thought of a child manifest themselves in *all* aspects of children's thinking. A change along one irrelevant dimension always seems to imply changes in the relevant dimensions for the preoperational child. The reverse is true for older counterparts who develop schemata that permit conservation.

The picture of conservation presented here is somewhat oversimplified. A child does not develop conservation schemata overnight in an all-or-nothing manner. Kamii

(1982) identifies three different levels or substages leading up to conservation of number. Conservation concepts are acquired slowly after much experience and subsequent assimilation and accommodation. Qualitatively new patterns of responses are interpreted by Piaget to reflect newly formed or reorganized schemata (cognitive structures).

The acquisition of schemata that permit conservation does not take place at the same time in all areas. The application of conservation principles to different kinds of problems usually follows a sequence. Conservation of number is always attained before other conservation skills, and conservation of volume is usually attained last. The structures permitting conservation are typically acquired at the following ages:

Conservation	Age
number	5–6
substance (mass)	7–8
area	7–8
liquid volume	7–8
weight	9–10
volume (solids)	11–12

Such a developmental sequence suggests that the ability to conserve liquid volume always implies the ability to conserve area, substance, and number. Each new kind of conservation always implies that previous levels in the sequence have been attained.[8]

Piaget and his collaborators conducted and published research on children's acquisition of conservaton concepts almost continuously from 1937 until 1977 (Easley 1978). Many dozens of studies were carried out by the Geneva group to more thoroughly understand the conservation phenomenon. In addition, hundreds of research studies were conducted by scholars in various countries interested in conservation. Not all psychologists agreed with Piaget's interpretation of his research, nor with the assumptions he made in his theory.

Piaget contended that conservation abilities evolve "naturally" out of the experiences most children have. Children tend to develop conservation abilities at about the same age, and tend to develop different conservation operations in an invariant sequence. In most cultures, children without formal schooling attain conservation as readily as children with schooling.[9] Direct teaching of conservation skills to preoperational children is not generally successful.

According to Piagetian theory, the interpretation of these findings is that conservation abilities will not emerge until cognitive structures (schemata) evolve that make true conservation responses possible. Changes in schemata come about only after considerable assimilation and accommodation of experience. A child must attain reversibility, must learn to de-center perceptions, and must follow transformations. He or she must become less egocentric and learn to question his or her thinking. These changes all come about gradually and are prerequisites to the development of the schemata permitting conservation.

AFFECTIVE DEVELOPMENT: THE EMERGENCE OF RECIPROCITY AND MORAL FEELINGS

Reciprocity of Feelings

The first social feelings arise during the preoperational stage. Representation and particularly spoken language are instrumental in the development of social feelings. Representation allows for the creation of images of experiences, including affective experiences. Thus, for the first time, feelings can be represented and recalled (remembered).[10] In this way, affective experiences come to last longer than the experiences themselves.

happy

> Representation and language allow feelings to acquire a stability and duration they have not had before. Affects, by being represented, last beyond the presence of the object that excites them. This ability to conserve feelings makes interpersonal and moral feelings possible. (Piaget 1981, p. 44)

During the sensori-motor stage, past events and experiences cannot be reconstructed because they are not represented by the child. With the capacity for reconstruction of the cognitive and affective past, behavior can assume an element of consistency that was not possible before representation. With the reconstructed past an element in current behavior, affect is less tied to immediate experience and perception than it previously was. Behavior can become a bit more stable and predictable. Feelings have the potential of becoming more consistent as development in the stage proceeds. Thus, where the sensori-motor child may "like" an object or person one day but not the next, the preoperational child typically shows more consistency in liking and disliking when the past is remembered and taken into account in the present.

Piaget contends that the basis for social interchange is a *reciprocity* of attitudes and values between the young child and others.

obnoxious

These considerations lead us to see liking other people not so much as the consequences of the enrichment that each partner draws from the other but as a reciprocity of attitudes and values. (Piaget 1981, pp. 45-46)

This form of exchange—reciprocity—leads, or can lead, to each party valuing the other person (mutual respect). Each is appreciated by the other in some way. In subsequent interactions, the values derived through reciprocal actions are not lost but are represented and "remembered." Because these prior value placements are retained, as representations, future interchanges are more likely to anticipate positive (or negative) affective experiences.

First Moral Feelings

Piaget studied the development of moral *reasoning* in children. He viewed the development of moral reasoning as an aspect of social development. Moral feelings, for Piaget, were feelings that have "to do with what is necessary and not just what is desirable or preferable to do" (Piaget 1981, p. 55).

He suggested that moral norms have three characteristics:

. . . (a) a moral norm is generalizeable to all analogous situations, not just to identical ones; (b) a moral norm lasts beyond the situation and conditions that engender it; and (c) a moral norm is linked to a feeling of autonomy. (Ibid.)

He indicated that these norms or characteristics of moral reasoning are not fully in place until the concrete operational stage.

From two to seven years, none of these conditions is met. To begin with, norms are not generalized but are valid only under particular conditions. For example, the child considers it wrong to lie to his parents and other grown-ups but not to his comrades. After the age of eight, however, children understand that it is wrong to lie in any situation, and they argue in a valid way that lying to one's comrades is more serious. Second, instructions remain linked to certain represented situations analagous to perceptual configurations. An instruction, for example, will remain linked to the person who gave it, or children will judge that a lie is "not as naughty" if the person duped is unaware he has been lied to. . . . Finally, there is no autonomy during the preoperational period. "Good" and "bad" are defined as that which conforms or fails to conform to the instructions one has received. (Ibid., pp. 55–56)

During the preoperational stage moral reasoning is viewed as prenormative. But moral reasoning during this stage is a clear advance over the capabilities of the sensori-motor child. Children's concepts of rules, accidents, lying, and justice are outlined briefly in the pages that follow.

CHILDREN'S CONCEPTS OF RULES

To investigate children's understanding of rules, Piaget (1965) asked children questions about the rules of a child's game. As mentioned earlier, the game was marbles, which requires two or more players. Piaget viewed marbles as an appropriate activity for study because it was a social game with a structure of rules. The rules vary from place to place, but there are always rules. Marbles was, and is, a popular game among children in Geneva.

Piaget interviewed twenty boys and girls, age 4-13 years, regarding their understanding of the rules. The questions that Piaget directed to the children were designed to determine whether the rules of the game were externally determined, just, and alterable. Thus, typical questions were "What are the rules [of marbles]?" "Show me how to play." "Can you invent a new rule?" and "Is it a fair rule?" In these interviews with children the experimenter functions both as a participant and an observer. The experimenter actually plays the game with the children in order to learn their way of playing (Gruber and Voheche 1977, pp. 156–157).

> The experimenter speaks more or less as follows. "Here are some marbles. . . . You must show me how to play. When I was little I used to play a lot, but now I've quite forgotten how to. I'd like to play again. Let's play together. You'll teach me the rules and I'll play with you." . . . You must avoid making any sort of suggestions. All you need do is to appear completely ignorant [about the game of marbles] and even make intentional mistakes so that the child may each time point out clearly what the rule is. Naturally, you must take the whole thing very seriously, all through the game. Then you ask who has won, and why, and if everything is not quite clear, you begin a new set. (Piaget 1965, p. 24)

In addition to questions about the rules, Piaget asked children to give the reasoning behind their answers. As we have seen, it is children's reasoning rather than their answers per se that usually provides the most information about their knowledge and concepts.

Piaget found that there were four broad stages in the development of children's knowledge of the rules of marbles. These stages parallel Piaget's four stages of cognitive development and are summarized here as the (1) motor stage, (2) egocentric stage, (3) stage of cooperation, and (4) stage of codification of rules.

Stage 1: Motor Stage. In Piaget's first stage of comprehension of rules, the motor stage, a child is not aware of any rules. During the first few years of life, and frequently extending into the preoperational stage of cognitive development, marbles are played with according to habit and in any way the child wants. At this stage, children play with marbles by themselves. The activity is nonsocial. Marbles are primarily objects to be explored (physical knowledge). A child's enjoyment seems to come largely from the motoric or muscular manipulation of the marbles. There is no evidence of any awareness of a game in the social sense.

Stage 2: Egocentric Stage. Usually between age 2 and age 5, children become aware of the existence of rules and begin to want to "play the game" with other, usually older, children. Young children begin by imitating older children's play, but the cognitively egocentric child continues to play *by himself or herself*, without trying to "win." In the same way, children's early preoperational use of spoken language is characterized by asocial collective monologues (egocentric); their play in groups is characterized by a lack of any social interaction or true cooperation. Piaget's observation helps illustrate the point.

> Loeff (5) often pretends to be playing with Mae [another boy] ... he immediately begins to "fire" at the marbles assembled in a heap and plays without either stopping or paying any attention to us. "Have you won?—*I don't know, I think I have.*—Why?—*Yes, because I threw the mibs* [marbles]—and I?—*Yes, because you threw the mibs.*" (Ibid., p. 38)

At this stage of reasoning about rules, children believe everyone can win. Rules are viewed as fixed, and respect for them is unilateral.

What seems to be asocial behavior, egocentrism, and isolated play is actually an advance over the behavior of the previous stage from a social point of view. The child wants to play with other children and attempts to adapt socially by imitating other children. Still, the egocentric child typically lacks any appreciation or knowledge of the game from a social point of view. Such children imitate what they see, but do not yet reason like their older playmates. Thus their "play" does not involve cooperation. There is no autonomy of reasoning. But because adaptations are attempted, their behavior represents an advance over the behavior of the earlier stage.

It is usually not until age 7 or 8 (stage 3) that children begin to cooperate socially in playing games. Around this time there is usually a clearer understanding of the rules of the game. The object of the game for children becomes to win. Around eleven or twelve years of age (stage 4), most children come to understand that rules are, or can be, made by the group; the group can change rules; and rules are necessary for fair play.

Stages 3 and 4 in the understanding of rules are dealt with in detail in the next two chapters.

Concepts of Accidents and Clumsiness

Parents and teachers of preschool and early elementary school children know that children frequently have difficulty viewing other children's accidents as "accidents." For example, one child may accidentally bump into another. The child who has been bumped typically views the act as intentional and worthy of appropriate retribution. Endless physical and verbal classroom scuffles are initiated by such accidents or clumsiness. Young children are unable to appreciate other children's *intentions* or to see another child's point of view (egocentrism), and parents and teachers are frustrated in their attempts to explain to young children that accidents and clumsiness on the part of others do not deserve punishment. The problem is that young children typically have not yet *constructed concepts of intentionality*. They firmly believe in the moral credo "an eye for an eye, and a tooth for a tooth," and in its application in all cases. Piaget's work suggests that until children construct a concept of intentionality, reasoning alone cannot dissuade them from retributive acts. They are simply not capable of understanding intentionality.

Piaget interviewed children to discover their concepts and beliefs about clumsiness and accidents. He used pairs of stories that contrasted children's intentions against the quantitative results of their "accidents." Children were asked to compare the accidents in two stories to decide which was worse and then to explain their selection. One pair of stories follows:

A. A little boy who is called John is in his room. He is called to dinner. He goes into the dining room.

But behind the door there was a chair, and on the chair was a tray with fifteen cups on it. John couldn't have known that there was all this behind the door. He goes in, the door knocks against the tray, bang go the fifteen cups and they all get broken!

B. Once there was a little boy whose name was Henry. One day when his mother was out he tried to get some jam out of the cupboard. He climbed up on a chair and stretched out his arms. But the jam was too high up and he couldn't reach it and have any. But while he was trying to get it he knocked over a cup. The cup fell down and broke. (Ibid., p. 122)

Piaget found that among children younger than age 7 or 8, the boy in the first story, John, is usually viewed as having committed a "worse" act. John's actions are typically viewed as worse than Henry's because John broke *15 cups* while Henry broke only *1 cup*. The children's judgments are based on the concrete or quantitative results of the actions. John broke more cups, and that's that! There is no appreciation yet of *intention* in judging actions. Motives are not considered.

Around age 8 or 9, with the construction of concepts related to intentionality, children typically *begin* to be able to consider events from someone else's point of view. This parallels a reduction in egocentric thought. Children begin to see that motives and intentions are *as important* as the results of actions. Piaget recorded the following responses and reasoning of a nine-year-old to the above stories.

Corm (9): *"Well, the one who broke them as he was coming isn't naughty, 'cos he didn't know there was any cups. The other one wanted to take the jam and caught his arm on a cup*—Which one is naughtiest?—*The one who wanted to take the jam.*—How many cups did he break?—*One.*—And the other boy?—*Fifteen.*—Which one would you punish most?—*The boy who wanted to take the jam. He knew, he did it on purpose."* (Ibid., p. 129)

Increasingly, intentions become more important to the child than the consequences of a particular action. This comes about only when children are able to view actions from the point of view of others. Children progress from a less social to a more social form of cooperative reasoning, similar in nature to their comprehension-understanding of rules.

Children and Lying

Another interesting social and moral topic Piaget investigated is the development of children's concepts about lying. Parents and teachers frequently observe a great deal of what they would call lying among young children. Understandably, this can be a source of great concern to adults. Many parents ask themselves if they are rearing a "liar." What Piaget learned about children's concepts of lying may help us understand these behaviors. In this research Piaget asked children questions to determine their definition of a lie, and why one should not lie.

What is a lie? Before age 6 or 7, most children view a lie as something that is "naughty." In addition, young children usually consider involuntary errors to be lies.

Nus (6): "What is a lie?—*It's when you say naughty words.*—Do you know any naughty words?—

Yes.—Tell me one.—*Charogne* [Corpse]. Is it a lie?—
Yes.—Why?—*Because you mustn't say naughty
words.*—When I say 'Fool!' is it a lie?—*Yes."* . . .

Rad (6): "*A lie is words you mustn't say, naughty
words."* . . .

Web (6): "Once there was a boy who didn't know
where the Rue des Acacias was [the street where
Web lives]. A gentleman asked him where it was. The
boy answered 'I think it's over there, but I'm not
sure.' And it wasn't over there! Did he make a mistake, or did he tell a lie?—*It was a lie.*—Did he make
a mistake?—*He made a mistake.*—Then it wasn't a
lie?—*He made a mistake and it was a lie."* (Ibid., pp.
143–44)

Between age 6 or 7 and age 10 or so, a lie is typically
viewed as something that is *not true*. A false statement is
viewed as a lie regardless of the intent. If it is not true, then
it is a lie.

Chap (7): "What is a lie?—*What isn't true, what
they say that they haven't done.*—Guess how old I
am.—*Twenty.*—No, I'm thirty. Was it a lie what you
told me?—*I didn't do it on purpose.*—I know. But is
it a lie all the same, or not?—*Yes, it is all the same,
because I didn't say how old you really were.*—Is it a
lie?—*Yes, because I didn't speak the truth.*—Ought
you to be punished?—*No.*—Was it naughty or not
naughty?—*Not so naughty.*—Why?—*Because I spoke
the truth afterwards!"* (Ibid., p. 144)

It is as if children define a lie as a moral fault. Only after
age 10 or 11 do children begin to recognize intentions in
relation to lying. At this level of reasoning a lie is defined
as something that is *intentionally false*. As we have seen with
the previous moral concepts, an appreciation of intentions
is not attained in most children until the development of
formal operations.

Why one should not lie. Piaget reported that when
questioned about why one should not lie, the reason typi-

cally given by children through age 7 or so was, "You get punished." A typical child's report follows:

> Zamb (6): "Why must we not tell lies?—*Because God punishes them.*—And if God didn't punish them?—*Then we could tell them.*" (Ibid., p. 168)

Punishment is the criterion used to determine whether a lie is permissible or not. According to young children, one does not tell a lie because of the punishment lying can bring. But if there is no punishment, it is perfectly acceptable to tell lies.

For the older child, after age 9 or so, there is a separation of the concept of lie from punishment. At this point in development children typically believe that a lie is wrong even if it goes unpunished.

> Girl (9): "Why is it naughty [a lie]?—*Because we get punished.*—If you didn't know you had told a lie, would it be naughty too?—*It would be naughty, but less naughty. . . . Why would it be naughty?—Because it is a lie all the same.*" (Ibid., p. 169)

Here the rule is viewed by the child as obligatory and independent of punishment. There is clearly an element of cooperation in the child's reasoning, although rules are still seen as imposed by authorities on children rather than an integral part of cooperation.

Piaget observed that a maturing of children's concepts about lying generally occurs around age 10–12. Intentions become the major critieria used to evaluate lying. The older child also recognizes that *not lying* is necessary for social cooperation. Children come to oppose lying because "truthfulness" is necessary for cooperation. Once again, there is a shift from a morality of contraint to a morality of cooperation.

> In the first place, a lie is wrong because it is
> an object of punishment; if the punishment were
> removed, it would be allowed. Then a lie becomes

something that is wrong in itself and would remain
so even if the punishment were removed. Finally, a
lie is wrong because it is in conflict with mutual
trust and affection. Thus the consciousness of lying
gradually becomes interiorized and the hypothesis
may be hazarded that it does so under the influence
of cooperation. (Ibid., p. 171)

Young children's "lies" are frequently spontaneous and
not designed to deceive.

. . . the tendency [in young children] to tell lies is
a natural tendency, so spontaneous and universal
that we can take it as an essential part of the child's
egocentric thought. In the child, therefore, the problem of lies is the clash of the egocentric attitude with
the moral constraint of the adult. (Ibid., p. 139)

The egocentric child frequently alters the truth
according to his or her desires. Lying is viewed as "bad"
by the young child *if it is punished by adults*. On the other
hand, the child who has some expectation that lying will
go unpunished sees nothing morally wrong with lying.

Punishment and Justice

In Piaget's research on the development of children's
concepts of justice, and more specifically on their concepts
of punishment, two distinct kinds of punishment emerge.
The concept of punishment Piaget observed in young children he called *expiatory* punishment. Expiatory punishment is strong punishment, administered to children by
parents or other adult authorities for breaking rules. The
general reasoning children use to support the use of expiatory punishment as "just" is that "painful" punishment
will deter further rule breaking. Expiatory punishment is
arbitrary in character because it does not bear any relationship to the "crime." For example, a boy who did not clean
up his room after being told to do so is punished by not
being allowed to go to a movie. Or a child is sent on an

important errand by the parent but does not carry out the request. The child is punished by not being allowed to play in the next school baseball game. In both cases, the punishments are not related to the *content* of the rule broken. Had the first boy been deprived of the use of everything in the room he did not clean up, the punishment would not be arbitrary (regarding the content). Expiatory punishment is always handed out by authorities, always involves constraint, and usually is arbitrary with respect to rules broken.

The second major punishment sanctioned by children Piaget called punishment *by reciprocity*. Punishment by reciprocity assumes there is no need for "painful" punishment to gain adherence to rules. The person who breaks the rules must simply be made aware that breaking rules destroys the social relationship and the basic social contract of cooperation. This awareness, in itself, is believed to generate sufficient "grief" to restore and ensure cooperation. If material or social punishment is necessary, the punishment *is not arbitrary* (as is expiatory punishment). Punishment on the basis of reciprocity is *always* related in some way to the *content* of the rule broken. For example, the boy who did not clean up his room after being told to do so may be deprived of the objects (toys, clothes, books, and the like) he did not clean up. Or the child who did not perform a requested errand is denied similar help by his parents when the child requests it. These punishments are "natural consequences" of rule breaking and presumably help to point out to children the consequences of their actions. While there can be a strong element of coercion in punishment by reciprocity, the emphasis is on persuasion and prevention rather than on punishment for its own sake. Punishment by reciprocity is guided by principles of cooperation and equality rather than adult authority and constraint.

Piaget investigated children's concepts of justice by telling them stories about children who did things they were not supposed to do and asking which forms of punishment were most appropriate or just. Here is one of the stories:

> A little boy is playing in his room. His mother
> asks him to go and fetch some bread for dinner

because there is none left in the house. But instead of going immediately the boy says that he can't be bothered, that he'll go in a minute, etc. An hour later he has not gone. Finally, dinner time comes, and there is no bread on the table. The father is not pleased and he wonders which would be the fairest way of punishing the boy. He thinks of three punishments. The first would be to forbid the boy to go to the Roundabouts [fair] the next day. . . . The second punishment the father thought of was not to let the boy have any bread to eat. (There was a little bread left from the previous day.) . . . The third punishment the father thinks of is to do to the boy the same thing as he had done. The father would say to him, "You wouldn't help your mother. Well I am not going to punish you, but the next time you ask me to do anything for you, I shall not do it, and you will see how annoying it is when people do not help each other." (The little boy thinks this would be all right, but a few days later his father would not help him reach a toy he could not get by himself. The father reminded him of his promise.) . . . Which of these three punishments was the fairest? (Ibid., p. 202)

Children between six and twelve years of age were told four stories and asked to judge which punishments were fairest and to give their *reasoning* for their judgments. Children were also asked to rate the punishments according to their severity. The responses children gave to the stories were classified as punishment by either reciprocity or expiation, and the frequencies for different ages were determined. Piaget found a distinct increase in children's preference for punishment by reciprocity with increase in age (see Table 4.1). Although some children at all ages recommended expiatory punishment as most appropriate, and some recommended punishment by reciprocity, a clear trend is evident. Younger children favor expiatory punishment; older children favor punishment by reciprocity.

Ang (6) repeats story . . . correctly: "How should he be punished?—*Shut him up in a room.*—What will that do to him?—*He'd cry.*—Would that be

Table 4.1
Age and Preferred Punishment

Age	Percent of Children Preferring Punishment by Reciprocity
6–7	28
8–10	49
11–12	82

fair?—*Yes.*" He is then told of the three possible punishments: "Which is the fairest?—*I'd have not given him his toy.*—Why?—*He'd been naughty.*—Is that the best of the three punishments?—*Yes.*—Why?—*Because he was very fond of his toy.*—Is that the fairest?—*Yes.*" Thus it is not the principle of reciprocity that carries the day, it is the idea of the severest punishment. . . .

Zim (6): Zim does not think much of the last two punishments. The third "*is not hard.*—Why?—*On the little boy.*—Why is it not hard on him?—*It isn't much.*—The second is also '*not much.*'" The fairest therefore is the first "because he's not on the Roundabouts [at the fair]." (Ibid., p. 211)

Among younger children, the fairest punishment is the harshest; the punishments selected are arbitrary. It is clear that younger children believe in the need for severe punishment. As children develop, Piaget found that their concepts of justice change gradually. About half the children Piaget interviewed between the ages of eight and ten made judgments based on reciprocity and abandoned a criterion based on severity of punishment (expiatory punishment).

Baum (9): "*The last [punishment] is the best. Since the boy won't help, well his mother won't help him either.*—And which is the fairest of the other two punishments?—*Not to give him any bread, then he'd have nothing to eat at supper, because he wouldn't help his mother.*—And the first?—*That was the one he deserved least. He wouldn't have minded. He'd still have been able to play with his toys and he would have had bread in the evening."* ...

Nus (11): *"I'd have given him a smacking."* The father thought of three punishments. (I tell them to him.) "Which do you think is the fairest?—*Not to give him any help.*—Do you think it is fairer than smacking him?—*Fairer.*—Why?—(He hesitates.) ... *Because it's doing about the same thing to him as he had done.*—And of the other two, which is the fairest?—*Not to let him have any bread.*—Why?—*Because he didn't fetch any."* (Ibid., pp. 215-16)

These interviews demonstrate that the older children Piaget interviewed view neither severe nor arbitrary punishment as the most appropriate. For these children, punishment based on reciprocity is more "just" than punishment based on expiation. The emphasis is clearly on punishment that "fits the crime" and helps the child realize the social consequences of his actions. Older children's judgments as to which punishments are most appropriate seem to focus more on prevention and less on retaliation than do the judgments of younger children.

The preoperational stage is the time when moral concepts begin to develop. Children begin to be aware that some things are necessary to do even if they are not desirable to do. Children become aware of rules during this stage.

Initially they view rules as fixed and unchangeable, and as having been passed down by some authority.

Preoperational children do not have concepts of intentionality and fail to take the intentions of others into account. Thus the "accidents" of other children are rarely viewed as accidents.

For preoperational children, justice tends to be equated with punishment and whatever adults say is right must be right. Again, lacking concepts of intentionality, children judge lies to be what authority says are lies. Throughout this stage, there is no evidence of *autonomy* in reasoning.[11]

SUMMARY

Qualitatively, the thought of the preoperational child is an advance over the thought of the sensori-motor child. Preoperational thought is no longer primarily restricted to immediate perceptual and motor events. Thought is truly representational (symbolic); and behavior sequences can be played out in the head rather than only in real physical events. Even so, perception still dominates reasoning. When conflicts arise between perception and thought, as in conservation problems, children using preoperational reasoning make judgments based on perception.

The preoperational stage is marked by some dramatic attainments. Language is acquired very rapidly between the ages of 2 and 4. Behavior in the early part of the period is largely egocentric and nonsocial. These characteristics become less dominant as the stage proceeds, and by age 6 or 7 children's conversations become largely communicative and social.

While preoperational thought is an advance over sensori-motor thought, it is restricted in many respects. The child is unable to reverse operations, and cannot follow transformations; perceptions tend to be centered; and the child is egocentric. These characteristics make for slow, concrete, and restricted thought. During this stage, thought is still largely under the control of the immediate and the perceptual, as can be seen in the typical preoperational child's inability to solve conservation problems. As cognitive development proceeds, so too does affective development. Representation and language development facilitate the beginnings of true social behavior. Moral feelings and moral reasoning make their appearance, but only in limited forms. Children begin to be able to reason about rules and justice, but without having developed concepts such as intentionality. Autonomy is absent during preoperational reasoning.

Cognitive development and affective development are not arrested from age 2 to age 7. Rather, they move steadily along, assimilation and accommodation resulting in the constant evolution of new and improved cognitive machinery (schemata). The preoperational child's behavior is initially like that of the sensori-motor child. By age 7, there is little resemblance.

NOTES

1. Other than spoken language, forms of representation that preoperational children use and comprehend include drawings, some symbols, and pictures and their internal "images." The use and comprehension of some written forms of representation, such as letters, written words, and numbers, develop later.

2. Forms of representation that are arbitrary and bear no likeness to what they represent (letters, words, numbers) are called *signs* by Piaget. Forms of representation that in part look like what they represent he calls *symbols*.

3. In some cases where children do not learn to speak between the ages of 2 and 4, the reason may be that there was not any adaptation value for them to do so. One example is of a three-and-a half-year-old boy who used little speech and was suspected of being retarded. An investigation determined that the boy's mother was extremely good at anticipating the boy's every need and did so effectively. Every need was met. There was little need for the boy to speak or learn to speak. Other examples can be found in Wadsworth 1978.

4. Children raised in bilingual homes learn two languages at the same time without any apparent increase in effort. Until about age 5, children tend to mix the two languages in their talking. They use the words of each interchangeably though they have

no difficulty understanding either language when it is spoken to them. Sometime around age 5, they realize they are dealing with two different, if parallel, codes and rapidly begin to unmix the two in their talking.

5. Piaget developed a procedure for assessing children's levels of knowledge with respect to a particular concept. This is called the clinical interview. In this procedure a child is presented with a concrete problem or a verbal question and asked questions relative to the concept of interest. Children's responses, whether correct or incorrect, are always followed by a request for reasons for their answers. This may be followed by more questions and requests for reasoning. The examiner's objective is to understand the child's concept (of number). Thus, questions are frequently made up "on the spot" in response to children's previous answers. The clinical interview relative to a particular concept is ended only when the examiner is satisfied that the child's level of understanding of the concept has been identified.

In this process, the examiner makes inferences about the child's comprehension from his or her reasoning. The reasoning the child gives is at least as important as the answers. Children can provide correct answers ("both rows have the same number") and have incorrect reasoning ("I guessed" or "I thought you were trying to trick me, so I didn't say what I thought"). Both correct answers and correct reasoning are necessary to conclude that the child has contructed the concept.

A more complete discussion of Piaget's clinical method and procedures for assessment can be found in Wadsworth 1978. For Piaget's original discussion of the procedure see Piaget 1963a.

6. Farm children may answer this question differently based on their experience. For example, some children indicate that the cow in the field with two adjacent barns has more grass to eat than the cow in the field with two separated barns. Their reasoning sometimes is that the area of grass next to barns is usually negligible or unfit to eat, and since the adjacent barns have fewer sides to the field, there is more edible grass in that field. From this reasoning it cannot be concluded that they do not have the conservation of area concept.

7. Liquid problems are usually solved after age 7 or 8. More sophisticated volume conservation problems, such as those requiring the measurement of displaced water when an object is immersed, are not solved until about age 12 (Piaget and Inhelder 1969, p. 98).

8. Under the guidance of competent and trained persons, problems like conservation problems and others can be used to

assess children's intellectual development from a Piagetian point of view. They can also be used to determine a child's level of development regarding a particular concept. Many professionals feel that a Piagetian methodology provides a substitute for, or a supplement to, conventional intelligence testing because Piagetian methods *clearly* measure reasoning, logical thought, and knowledge. Competency in making valid assessments takes time and training. Those interested in learning more about how to make such assessments can consult works that deal with Piagetian assessment in detail (for example, Wadsworth 1978; Piaget 1963a; Copeland 1974).

9. This should not be interpreted to mean that children learn regardless of whether they go to school. It means only that cognitive structures (schemata) will evolve in most cases regardless of whether children go to school. Chapter 8 deals with this in more detail.

10. According to Piaget, what we can recall or remember is *not* an exact replica of the object or action being remembered. What is "remembered" is derived from the representation (image) of the object or event that we have. Representations are not mirror images of objects and events. Images are imitations shaped by the cognitive and perceptual capabilities of the individual at the time they are created. What is "remembered" is reconstructed from the images available. Thus, when we talk of feelings being remembered, we are talking of reconstructions from images of feelings, not the feelings themselves.

11. Autonomy means being governed by oneself and one's reasoning rather than by others (Kamii 1982). In addition, autonomy means being able to make decisions oneself; it means being able to evaluate situations using one's moral and cognitive reasoning. A sense of duty to one's values is implied. See Kamii 1982; Piaget 1973.

Chapter 5

THE STAGE OF CONCRETE OPERATIONS

Whether one conceives of development as proceeding along a continuum or in a spiraling continuum (Gallagher and Reid 1981), the important point is that progress between stages is continuous, as are changes within stages. There are no abrupt changes.[1]

During the stage of concrete operations (age 7–11), a child's reasoning processes become logical. He or she develops what Piaget called *logical operations*. Piaget said that an intellectual operation "is an internalized system of actions that is fully reversible" (1981, p. 59). That is, the child evolves logical thought processes (operations) that can be applied to problems that exist (are concrete). Unlike the child who is preoperational, the child at the stage of concrete operations has no trouble solving conservation problems and providing correct reasoning for his or her answers. When faced with a discrepancy between thought and perception, as in conservation problems, the concrete operational child makes cognitive and logical decisions, as opposed to perceptual decisions. The child is no longer perception bound and becomes able, typically between the ages of 7 and 11, to do all the cognitive operations that limit the intellectual activity of the preoperational child. The concrete operational child *de-centers* his or her perceptions and attends to *transformations*. Most important, the concrete operational child attains *reversibilty* of mental operations. In addition, cooperative, nonegocentric communication evolves. For the first time, the child becomes a truly social being.

The quality of concrete operational thought surpasses that of preoperational thought. Schemata for the logical operations of seriation and classification appear. Improved concepts of causality, space, time, and speed evolve. In essence, the concrete operational child attains a level of intellectual activity that is superior in all respects to that of the preoperational child.

While a concrete operational child evolves a functional use of logic not evidenced in the behavior of younger children, he or she does not attain the highest level of use of logical operations. Here the term *concrete* (as in concrete operations) is significant. While the child clearly evolves logical operations, these operations (reversibility, classification, and so on) are only useful in solving problems involving concrete (real, observable) objects and events in the immediate present (Piaget 1972a). For the most part, concrete operational children cannot yet apply logic to problems that are hypothetical, purely verbal, or abstract. In addition, they cannot correctly reason about concrete problems that involve many variables. If concrete operational children are presented with a purely verbal problem, they are usually unable to solve it correctly. If the same problem is presented in terms of real objects, they can apply logical operations and solve the problem if there are no multiple variables involved. Thus, the concrete operational stage can be viewed as being a transition between prelogical (preoperational) thought and the completely logical thought of older children.

HOW CONCRETE OPERATIONAL THOUGHT DIFFERS FROM PREOPERATIONAL THOUGHT

The preoperational child's thought is characterized by the dominance of perception over reasoning, and by egocentrism, centration, an inability to follow transformations, and an inability to reverse operations. These obstacles to logical thought are reflected in the preoperational child's inabilty to solve conservation problems. In contrast, concrete operational thought is free of all the characteristics that dominated preoperational thought. The typical concrete operational child can solve conservation problems. His (or her) thought is less egocentric; he can decenter his perceptions; he can follow transformations; and most important, he can reverse operations. When conflicts arise between perception and reasoning, the concrete operational child makes judgments based on reasoning. These characteristics are discussed in the pages that follow.

Egocentrism and Socialization

The preoperational child's thinking was dominated by egocentrism, an inability to assume the viewpoint of others, and the lack of a need to seek validation of her (or his) own thoughts. The concrete operational child's thinking is not egocentric in this respect. She is aware that others can come to conclusions that are different from hers, and as a consequence she is more likely to seek validation of her thoughts. In this respect the concrete operational child is liberated from the intellectual egocentrism of the previous period.

According to Piaget, liberation from egocentrism comes about primarily through social interaction with peers,[2] as the child is forced to seek verification of ideas.

> What then gives rise to the need for verification? Surely it must be the shock of our thoughts coming into contact with that of others, which produces doubt and the desire to prove. . . . The social need to share the thoughts of others and to communicate our own with success is at the root of our need for verification. Proof is the outcome of argument. . . . Argument is, therefore, the backbone of verification. (Piaget 1928, p. 204)

The concrete operational child does not display the egocentrism of thought characteristic of the preoperational child. At the stage of concrete operations, the use of language becomes almost completely communicative in function. Concepts are verified or denied through social interaction. As said previously, the socialization of behavior is a continuous process that begins in early childhood with simple imitations. Social behavior, by its very nature, is an important source of disequilibrium. Coming to look at something from another's viewpoint, questioning one's reasoning, and seeking validation from others are all essentially acts of accommodation.

With the development of concrete operations, language becomes less egocentric. Collective monologues, characteristic of children's speech before age 6 or 7 are largely absent. Children exchange information with one another in their conversations and learn to view events from the position of others.

Centration

The preoperational child's thinking is characterized by centration. Perceptions of events tend to center on single or limited perceptual aspects of a stimulus and do not take into account all the salient features of the stimulus. Thus, as we saw in the conservation of number problems, preoperational children tend to center on the length of stimulus configurations. The concrete operational child's thinking is not characterized by centering. Concrete thought becomes *de-centered*. De-centering is one of the abilities found in concrete thought that permits logical solutions to concrete problems.

Transformation

The preoperational child was unable to focus and coordinate on successive steps in a transformation. Each step in a transformation was viewed as independent of each successive step. There was no awareness or attention paid to the sequence or transformation involved.

The concrete operational child attains a functional understanding of transformations. He or she can solve problems involving concrete transformations and is aware of, and understands, the relationship between successive steps.

Reversibility

Preoperational thought lacks reversibility. Concrete operational thought is reversible. The difference between the two levels of thought can be seen in the following illustration of *inversion* from Piaget 1967 (p. 31). A child is shown three balls of the same size but each of a different color, marked *A*, *B*, *C* (see Figure 5.1). The balls are placed in a cylinder in the order *C*, *B*, *A*. The preoperational child correctly predicts that the balls will exit from the bottom of the cylinder in the same order: *C*, *B*, *A*. Once more the balls are in the cylinder in the same order. Then the cylinder is rotated 180 degrees. A preoperational child continues to predict that the balls will exit from the bottom of the tube in the same order as before: *C*, *B*, *A*. He or she is surprised when they exit in the order *A*, *B*, *C*. This is an example of the inability of preoperational thought to reverse operations and use the form of reversibility called *inversion*. A concrete operational child has no trouble with the above

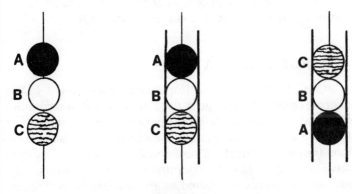

FIGURE 5.1

problem.[3] He or she can invert the change and make the appropriate deduction. Inversion is one of two primary forms of reversibility.

The second kind of reversibility that concrete operational children use is *reciprocity*. In response to the conservation of liquid problem (page 90), some concrete operational children argue that when liquid is poured into a taller but thinner container, the quantity of liquid does not change because the increased height is compensated for by the narrowness of the container (width compensates height). This is reasoning with *reciprocity*, or by compensation, and is the second form of reversibility found in concrete operational reasoning.[4]

Conservation

A hallmark of preoperational thought is the child's inability to conserve. With the attainment of concrete operations, the ability to reason logically about and solve conservation problems emerges. The related abilities to de-center, to follow transformations, and to reverse operations by inversion and reciprocity are all instrumental in developing conservation skills and advancing reasoning. A child becomes able to solve conservation of number problems around age 6 or 7. Conservation of area and mass problems are usually solved by age 7 or 8. Conservation of volume problems (measurement of displaced water when an object is immersed) are not solved correctly until age 11 or 12.

LOGICAL OPERATIONS

Cognitively, the most important development of the concrete operational stage is the attainment (construction) of logical operations. Logical operations are internalized cognitive actions that permit a child to arrive at conclusions that are "logical." These actions are directed by cognitive activity rather than dominated by perceptions. Logical operations are constructed, as are all cognitive structures, out of prior structures as a function of assimilation and accommodation. Logical operations are means of organizing experience (schemata) that are superior to prior organization.

According to Piaget, an operation always has four characteristics: (1) It is an action that can be internalized or carried out in thought as well as materially; (2) it is reversible; (3) it always supposes some conservation, some invariance; and (4) it never exists alone but is always related to a system of operations (Piaget 1970a, pp. 21–22). Operations become truly logical during the concrete operational stage. Previous operations (at the preoperational stage) were prelogical, never meeting all the above criteria. One logical operation, already discussed, is reversibility. Two other structures central to concrete operations are *seriation* and *classification* (Piaget 1977a). These two logical operations are basic to the child's understanding of number concepts (Wadsworth 1978; Gallagher and Reid 1981).

Seriation: Ordering Objects According to Differences

Seriation is the ability to mentally arrange a set of elements accurately according to increasing or decreasing size, weight, or volume. The ability to seriate *length* develops throughout the preoperational and concrete operational stages. The task usually used by Piagetians to assess knowledge of seriation of length is a simple one. A child is presented with a set of approximately 10 sticks varying in length by small but perceptible differences (1/4 inch). The child is asked to order the sticks from the smallest to the largest. The examiner may show a properly arranged construction prior to asking the child to make his or her construction. Piaget's research discerns five levels in development of seriation of length knowledge.

At the first level, age 4 or earlier, children typically place some of the sticks in a construction, with no order discernible. At Level 2, children construct pairs comprised of a small stick and a large stick, but their constructions show no relationship between pairs. Any stick can be placed in relation to any other stick, but is not simultaneously related to 2 sticks. Four- and five-year-olds eventually begin to form groups of 3 sticks, but without any order between groups of sticks.

At the next level, which is transitional (between Level 2 and Level 3), advances are made and several partial coordinations are seen. Children age 5–7 years frequently align the tops of the sticks (as in Figure 5.2) while paying no attention to the alignment of the bottoms of the sticks. Some children successfully order 4 or 5 sticks in a set, but usually no more.

At Levels 3 and 4, children age 7–8 successfully order the set of 10 sticks (as in the model), but there are qualitative differences in method between the two levels. Level 3 children typically use a trial and error approach.

> The entire series is finally ordered but by an empirical grouping method, that is, with local errors and corrections afterwards. On the other hand, the subject has not mastered the transitivity problem. (Piaget 1977, p. 131)

At Level 3, the child is unable to order 3 or more sticks in order mentally, demonstrating a lack of *transitivity*.[5] If it is unclear whether a child can order the series mentally, he or she can be asked to place the sticks successively in order behind a visual screen. This requires a mental ordering of the series for successful construction.

At Level 4, children have no difficulty with the seriation task. The 10 sticks are ordered accurately without trial

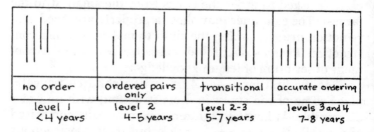

no order	ordered pairs only	transitional	accurate ordering
level 1 <4 years	level 2 4–5 years	level 2–3 5–7 years	levels 3 and 4 7–8 years

FIGURE 5.2

and error. Children employ strategies such as searching for the smallest stick, then the next smallest, and so on.

> This strategy implies both transitivity and the
> reversibility inherent in an operational structure:
> any stick is longer than all the proceeding ones and
> also shorter than all those that follow it in the series.
> (Gallagher and Reid 1981, p. 97)

Children at this level also have no difficulty with the visual blind problem. They are confident that their constructions are correct, even when they cannot see them.

Children's knowledge about seriation is constructed over a period of years. Each advance is a new equilibrium in the child's reasoning. Seriation of length is generally attained around age 7 or 8.[6]

Classification: Mentally Grouping Objects According to Similarities

In Piaget's traditional classification studies, children are presented with sets of objects (such as geometric shapes varying in size and color) and are asked to put the objects that are alike together (Piaget and Inhelder 1969; Piaget 1972b). Three levels of development emerge from these studies.

Level 1. Children of four or five years of age typically proceed by selecting objects to go together based on similarities. But the criterion they use is what is similar between two objects at a time. Thus, a child may put together a black circle and a white circle (both circles), then may add a white triangle to the white circle (both white), then may place a gray triangle with the white triangle (both triangles), insisting that they all go together (Figure 5.3). Objects are assimilated to similarities between individual pairs of objects only. Differences between objects in the set are ignored. There is no plan for the total set.

Level 2. Through age 7, children typically form collections of like objects along one dimension. That is, circles

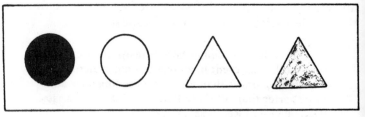

FIGURE 5.3

are put together, triangles are put together, and so on, when children are classifying by shape. If children are classifying by color, they will put black circles and black triangles together. Missing at this level of reasoning is any awareness of the *relationships between* collections or subcollections. Children at this level do not understand the logical relationship between a class and a subclass—or *class inclusion*.

In the typical class inclusion task, a child is presented with 20 brown wooden beads and 2 white wooden beads (Figure 5.4). After the child agrees that the beads are all wooden and 20 are brown and 2 are white, the following kind of question is asked: "Are there more wooden beads or more brown beads?" (Piaget 1952a).

Level 2 children typically respond that there are more brown beads than wooden beads. Their reasoning reflects that they compare the classes of brown and white and are unable to compare the subclass of brown beads to the larger class of wooden beads. These children do not understand class inclusion.

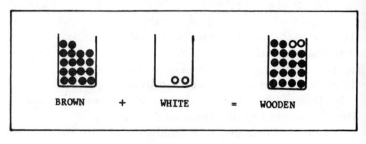

FIGURE 5.4

Level 3. Around age 8, children typically demonstrate an understanding of the class inclusion principle. Their reasoning on the class inclusion problem indicates that they understand that the class of brown beads must of necessity be smaller than the class of wooden beads. They consider *differences* (non-brown beads) as well as similarities in classification and are able to reason about the *relationships* between classes and subclasses.

Children's number concepts result from a synthesis of the logical operations of seriation and inclusion (Piaget and Inhelder 1969). Number concepts involve both order (seriation) and group membership (inclusion). The number concept "8" is a place in a series; and it is part of a set that includes 1, 2, 3, 4, 5, 6, 7, and 8.[7]

By now it should be clear to the reader that Piaget conceptualized cognitive development as occurring not in isolation but in all areas at the same time. A cognitive advance in one area affects other areas. With this in mind, let us consider the concrete operational child's concepts of causality, time, and speed.

Causality

Children's concepts of causality develop in the same manner that other concepts do. Development of causal concepts during the sensori-motor period was illustrated in Chapter 3. Piaget and Inhelder investigated children's concepts of causality in the following problem situation:

> . . . we once asked children from five to twelve what happens after lumps of sugar are dissolved in a glass of water. For children up to about seven, the dissolved sugar disappears and its taste vanishes like a mere odor; for children seven to eight its substance is retained without either its weight or its volume. After nine or ten, conservation of weight is present, and after eleven or twelve, there is also conservation of volume (recognizable in the fact that the level of water, which is slightly raised when the sugar is added, does not return to its initial level after the sugar is dissolved). (Ibid., p. 112)

As the above illustrates, children's causal concepts develop during the concrete operational stage. Qualitative changes in structures (schemata) are reflected in the development.

Time and Speed

Piaget and Inhelder contended that children typically do not understand the relationship between time and speed (velocity = speed/time) until age 10 or 11 (ibid., p. 103). Prior to this age, an object is considered to travel faster than another object only if it overtakes it while moving. When comparing the speeds of two objects, the preoperational child usually considers only the points of arrival and does not consider starting points and subsequent velocity or paths followed (ibid., p. 108). Consider the following: Two cars leave point *A* in Figure 5.5 at the same time. They both arrive at *B* at the same time, but they traverse different routes (1 and 2). After viewing this problem, observing the movement of the cars, the preoperational child reports that both cars traveled at the same speed. Not until age 8 or so does a ratio concept of speed in terms of the relationship between time and distance traveled begin to evolve.

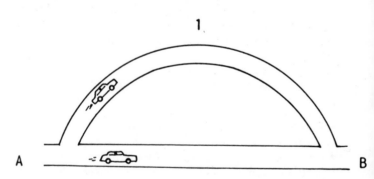

FIGURE 5.5

The concrete operational child's concepts of time and speed are superior to those of the preoperational child. Not until the stage of concrete operations do accurate concepts appear.

AFFECTIVE DEVELOPMENT: COOPERATION

Cognitive development and affective development are inseparable. Thus, when cognitive development and affective development are conceptualized independently, it is no surprise that there are clear parallels between the two.

In the concrete operational stage, reasoning and thought acquire greater stability than prevails in preoperational thought. The capability for reasoning becomes increasingly logical and less subject to influence by apparent perceptual contradictions. Reversibility of thought and de-centering help bring consistency and "conservation" to the concrete operational child's reasoning.

These factors influence not only cognitive reasoning but also affective reasoning. During the concrete operational stage, affect acquires a measure of stability and consistency that was not present earlier.

During the stage of concrete operations, internalized *reversible* operations (reversibility) appear in the child's affective reasoning. The origins of reversibility in affective life were seen in the preoperational stage. At that time, feelings were not fully "conserved," and affect was prenormative; but because day-to-day feelings could be represented and remembered, feelings were no longer unrelated.

Around age 7 or 8, there emerges *conservation of feelings* and values. Children become able to coordinate their affective thoughts from one event to another. What is preserved or conserved, over time, are some aspects of past feelings. Affective thought is now reversible. The past can be made a part of reasoning in the present through the ability to reverse and conserve.

Piaget suggested that social interaction during the preoperational stage encourages the development of conservation of feelings.

> ... social life requires thought to acquire a certain permanence. For this to occur, mental activity can no longer be represented in terms of personal symbols such as playful fantasies [symbolic play] but will have to be expressed in universal signifiers such as linguistic signs [language]. The uniformity and consistency of expression enforced by social life plays a large part, therefore, in the development of intellectual structures with their conservations and invariants; and it will lead to analogous transformations in the domain of feelings. In effect, the permanence obviously lacking from spontaneous feelings will appear with social and, especially, moral feelings. ...
>
> liking another person is a feeling that varies as long as it is spontaneous and linked to particular situations. It becomes lasting and reliable when feelings of *semi-obligation* are added. [italics added]
> (Piaget 1981, p. 60)

We noted in the last chapter that preoperational affect was prenormative. It did not meet fully any of the three criteria for being normative: (1) being generalizeable, (2) lasting beyond the moment, and (3) being linked to autonomy. During the concrete operational stage, these criteria are met as children's affective reasoning capabilities become "operational." In the same way that reversibility leads to a logic of thought, it leads to a logic of affect.[8] Internalized reversible operations appear in the affective domain.

To better understand Piaget's beliefs about affective development during the concrete operational stage it is important to understand his conceptualization of *the will* and *autonomy*.

The Will

Piaget asserted that "the affective analogue of intellectual operations is found in the act of will" (ibid., p. 61).

He viewed the will as a permanent scale of values constructed by the individual and to which he or she feels obliged to adhere. The will assumes the role of regulator (self-regulation) of affect and is thus the mechanism by which values are conserved. In cognitive activity, conflicts between perceptual experience and logical reasoning are regulated through conservation—the ability to maintain constancy in the face of logically irrelevant change. Similarly, conflicts between affective impulses are regulated by the will, once the will is developed. Once values are reasonably stable, and the will is in place, values can be asserted over conflicting impulses, even though the impulse may have been stronger at one point than the values and the will.

According to Piaget, a number of factors prompt the gradual development of the will. One factor, already mentioned, is the demand of social experience, which encourages a consistency in affective life. Behavior that has continuity is reinforced by others more than inconsistent behavior is. In addition, affective experiences and feelings are now conserved. At any given moment, the affective past—now represented in memory and the present—is a part of affective reasoning. The affective experiences of the past can no longer be disregarded. An awareness of past and present feelings can lead to different affective decisions than an awareness of only present feelings.[9]

Autonomy

Autonomy means being governed by oneself, not by others (Kamii 1982).[10] Autonomy of reasoning is reasoning according to one's own constructed set of norms. It evaluates, rather than automatically accepts the preformed values of others. In addition, autonomous reasoning considers others as well as the self.

During the preoperational stage, children view and accept rules as handed down from some higher authority—parents, God, the government. Justice is viewed in the light of living up to those rules. The child's morality at the preoperational level is one of obedience. Preoperational children do not reason about what is right or wrong. For them, what is right or wrong is predetermined (by authority) and not subject to their own evaluation. There is little cooperation in the social sense—there is only obedience.

Around age of 7 or 8, children *begin* to be capable of making their own moral evaluations. That is, they begin to reason about the "correctness" or "incorrectness" of actions and the effects of actions on others. This, of course, does not mean that their evaluations are necessarily correct; it means only that they begin to shift from a heteronomous morality of obedience to preformed values to a morality of cooperation and evaluation.

Mutual respect is an agent in the development of autonomous thought that appears during this stage. Until around age 7 or 8, children regard adults with unilateral respect (respect for authority). Children's morality is primarily one of obedience. Mutual respect is respect between "equals." Children can develop mutual respect only after they become able to see someone else's point of view.

One might suspect that mutual respect arises out of social pressures and experience. Piaget suggested that this is not the case, that social experience does not sufficiently explain this development. If anything, adult society usually encourages children to internalize unilateral respect for adult authority.[11]

Parents and teachers see early indicators of developing autonomy when children begin to come into conflict with adults over what is just and right. The seven-year-old who complains—claiming a lack of justice—that an older sibling got a bigger piece of cake or got to stay up an hour longer is frequently exhibiting autonomy of reasoning.

Autonomy is not fully developed during the concrete operational stage. Children's initial autonomous feelings are frequently from their perspective alone (egocentric). The same child in the above example who shows some autonomous reasoning when dealing with adults may not show any when dealing with siblings or peers—unless there is *mutual respect*. Further development is necessary before children become capable of taking all relevant factors into consideration and deciding what is the best course of action for all concerned and not simply for themselves.

With the development of the will and autonomy, clear shifts become evident in children's concepts of rules, accidents, lying, justice, and moral reasoning.

Rules

During the sensori-motor stage, children do not have concepts of rules for games. During the preoperational stage, children become aware of rules and demand of others a rigid adherence to rules. They view rules as fixed and permanent, and when they play games, they play to "win."

Usually around age 7 or 8 (the beginning of the concrete operational stage of reasoning), children begin to grasp the significance of rules for proper game playing. *Cooperation* in a social sense begins to emerge. Rules are no longer seen as absolute and unchangeable. Children typically develop the notion that the rules of the game can be changed if all agree to the change. Children begin to try to *win* (a social act) while conforming to the rules of the game.

> In seeking to win the child is trying above all to contend with his partners *while observing common rules*. The specific pleasure of the game ceases to be muscular [Stage 1] and egocentric [Stage 2] and becomes social. (Piaget 1965, p. 42)

For the child who is beginning to demonstrate cooperation, the aim of the game is no longer to knock the marbles out of the circle or square but to *win* (in a competitive sense).

While cooperation is evident in Stage 3 children, they typically do not know (have not constructed) the rules of the game in detail, and many discrepancies are apparent in children's reports of what rules are. This lack of agreement about the rules and the emphasis on winning can be observed in practically any group of young children engaged in a game. If permitted, they will spend more time arguing about what the rules are, in an effort to win, than they actually will spend playing the game.

Accidents and Clumsiness

Earlier it was noted that preoperational children are unable to consider the intention of others in their judgments about accidents. Thus the preoperational child who is accidentally bumped by another typically views the bumping as intentional rather than accidental. Similarly, the child who breaks 15 cups is naughtier than the child who breaks a single cup, regardless of either child's intentions. Fifteen broken cups are worse than one.

Around age 8 or 9, the typical child who is developing concrete operations begins to develop the ability to consider others' points of view. With this ability, intentions begin to be understood and considered when making judgments. Retribution is no longer automatically sought in the case of "accidents." Intentions become more important than the consequences of actions. The boy who broke 15 cups by accident is no longer viewed as "worse" than the boy who broke a single cup doing something he was told not to do.

Unfortunately, Piaget's view of children's understanding of accidents does not offer any hope that young children can be "taught" to understand other children's intentions. The understanding of intentions cannot be "taught" to young children through verbal methods. According to Piaget, each child must *construct* the concept out of his or her active interactions with others. Peers are particularly important in this process. Until a child becomes capable of taking the viewpoint of others, he or she cannot construct a concept of intentionality. Piaget's findings help us to understand young children's responses to the accidents and clumsiness of others, but they do not solve the problem of what to do about such behavior.[12]

Lying

We have seen that well into the concrete operational stage children view a lie as something that is *not true*. It is not until around age 10 or 11 that children begin to consider intentions when judging whether an act is a lie. At this level, untruths that are not intended to deceive are not automatically judged to be lies.

The "adult" concept of a lie is very different from that of the typical preoperational or early concrete operational child. Implicit in this difference is that most children cannot understand the adult conception of a lie before developing middle concrete operational thought. Even if they wish to, younger children cannot make adultlike judgments about lying.

> The child . . . is told not to lie long before he understands the social value of this order (for lack of sufficient socialization) and sometimes before he is able to distinguish intentional deception from the distortions of reality that are due to symbolic play or to simple desire. As a result, veracity (truth) is external to the personality of the subject and gives rise to moral realism and objective responsibility whereby a lie appears to be serious not to the degree that it corresponds to intent to deceive, but to the degree that it differs materially from the objective truth. (Piaget and Inhelder 1969, p. 126)

Justice

Piaget's research revealed that children's concepts of justice change as they develop. Preoperational children consider rules as fixed and unchangeable. "Just" punishments are harsh and frequently arbitrary (expiatory punishment). During the concrete operational stage, children develop a better, though not a complete, understanding of laws and rules. They begin to consider the role of intentions in deciding what is just. In addition, concrete operational children increasingly come to regard punishment by reciprocity as more appropriate than expiatory punishment.

Such is the case when a young girl is denied the use of objects scattered around her room after being instructed to clean them up and not doing so. The punishment in this instance is not arbitrary; it bears some relation to the punishable behavior.

As children develop affectively, changes can be seen in their moral reasoning. The development of normative affect, the will, and autonomous reasoning influence the moral and affective life of the concrete operational child. Children develop the capacity to "take the view of others," consider intentions, and better adapt to the social world.

SUMMARY

The stage of concrete operations is a transitional period between preoperational thought and formal (logical) thought. During the concrete operational stage, a child attains the use of fully logical operations for the first time. Thought is no longer dominated by perceptions, and the child is able to solve problems that exist or have existed (are concrete) in his or her experience.

The concrete operational child is not egocentric in thought in the way that preoperational children are. The child at the stage of concrete operations can assume the viewpoint of others, and spoken language is social and communicative. Such children can de-center perception and attend to transformations. Reversibility of thought is developed. Two important intellectual operations that develop are seriation and classification, which form the basis for number concepts.

Parallels can be observed between cognitive development and affective development during this stage. The development of the *will* allows for the regulation of affective reasoning. Autonomy of reasoning begins to develop, the child becoming increasingly an evaluator of arguments rather than an acceptor of preformed ideas. This leads to an understanding of intentionality and an increased capability of considering motives when making judgments. Growth can be seen in children's moral concepts, such as their understanding of rules, lying, accidents, and justice.

NOTES

1. Some readers of Piaget conclude that Piaget's stages are discrete and separate; for example, that a child goes to bed one night being preoperational and wakes up the next morning concrete operational. Nothing could be further from the truth. The progress is gradual, and over the years children develop from reasoning that is typical of the preoperational child to exhibiting reasoning that is typical of the concrete operational child.

2. Piaget called social interaction one of the variables that facilitate cognitive development. His writings suggest that social interactions are any behaviors (conversations, play, games, and so forth) that involve a real interchange between two or more persons. Thus, when language becomes functionally communicative, it is a form of social interaction.

3. The rotation of beads problem demonstrates simple reversibility. In 1977 Heard and Wadsworth found this form of reversibility to be attained, on average, late in the sixth year.

4. The argument by inversion for the conservation of liquid problem would be that if the liquid was poured back into its original container—from the tall, thin container—there would be the same amount of liquid.

5. Understanding *transitivity* is understanding that if A is less than B, and B is less than C, then A is necessarily less than C. Comprehension of transitivity is usually determined by using a problem similar to the following one: A child is presented with two sticks. One stick (A) is slightly shorter than the other stick (B). The child is asked to compare the two sticks and determine which stick is longer. The child is then shown stick B and a third stick

(C), which is slightly longer. Stick A is hidden from the child during the new comparison. The child is asked to compare sticks B and C. These first two comparisons are almost always accurate. With stick A still hidden, the child is asked to compare sticks A and C. To solve this problem, the child has to be able to mentally order the three sticks A, B, and C. Children typically develop transitive reasoning of this kind around age 7.

6. Different kinds of seriation learning, like different kinds of conservation learning, occur at different ages in an invariant sequence. Seriation of length is mastered usually at age 7 or 8 years. Seriation of weight (objects of the same size but different weights) is usually attained around age 9. Seriation of volume is not attained until about age 12 or so (Piaget, 1967).

The seriation task described has been used in studies on children's memory with interesting results (Piaget and Inhelder 1969). The 10-stick seriation task is presented and constructions noted. After a period of time (a week or more), the same children are asked to order the sticks again as they were asked to on the prior occasion. Again, performance is noted. Piaget and Inhelder found that many of the children's performance improved between the two occasions with improvement in their levels of development. They interpreted these results as indicating that "... memory causes the schemes corresponding to the child's level to predominate: the image-memory relates to this scheme rather than the perceptual model" (ibid., p. 82). The conclusion was that children remember what they understand rather than strictly what they see, and that memory (what they understand) can (will) improve over time if understanding improves.

7. For more on number concepts, see Wadsworth 1978; Kamii 1982; Copeland 1974.

8. Logic of affectivity may sound like a contradiction in terms. Piaget suggested that feelings are variable, and thus the behavior activated by feelings may be variable. When feelings begin to be "conserved," that is, to last from one situation to the next, a permanence underlying variable feelings emerges (1981, p. 60). A contradiction exists only if one asserts that feelings may not vary if they are to be logical: "... some people will say that moral feelings, however normative they may be, remain less universal, less stable, and less coercive than operational rules. This objection, in our opinion, is unfounded. If, in fact, some differences between logical and moral norms were to be found, it would be one of degree, not one of nature. On the whole, we believe this difference to be weaker than is ordinarily imagined. Common thought is at

least as far removed from operational norms as everyday behavior is from moral norms" (ibid., p. 61).

9. The existence of will does not mean that behavior is never "impulsive." The presence of the will merely indicates that one has the *capability* to reason about affective issues from a coordinated, reversible perspective. Many factors besides reasoning influence behavior. Thus it is not necessarily inconsistent to observe what seems to be impulsive behavior after the will is present.

10. Autonomy is discussed here in relation to affective development. The relevance of autonomy for cognitive development is elaborated in Chapter 8.

11. One objective frequently voiced by parents and educators is the development of "self-discipline." Self-discipline presumably is the control of one's behavior *by the self*. If Piaget is correct, self-discipline can most effectively be established through encouraging the development of moral autonomy and mutual respect. Indeed, it is questionable whether schools and parents functioning exclusively on a morality of unilateral respect can be a source of self-discipline.

12. The obvious implication in this situation is to realize that all children cannot understand intentions and consequently cannot respond to reasoning about intentions. This does not mean you have to excuse a child who hits another child who accidentally bumped into him. What it means is that you cannot expect the child to *understand* an argument that involves intentions. The only solution is to forbid children to hit other children, and to punish them when they do and reward them when they do not. On the other hand, some *accidents and their retributions* may be necessary in order for children to be prompted to construct the concepts involved. Young children typically understand that they themselves have accidents before they appreciate the accidents of others. Certainly the ability to take the view of another requires interactions.

Chapter 6

THE STAGE OF
FORMAL
OPERATIONS

During the stage of formal operations, which occurs around age 11–15 or older, a child develops the reasoning and logic to solve all classes of problems. There is a "freeing" of thought from direct experience. The child's cognitive structures reach maturity during this stage. That is, his or her potential quality of reasoning or thought (compared with the potential of "adult" thought) is at its maximum when formal operations are fully developed. After this stage, there are no further structural improvements in the quality of reasoning. The adolescent with fully developed formal operations typically has the cognitive *structural* equipment to think "as well as" adults. This does not mean that the thinking of the adolescent with formal reasoning is necessarily "as good as" adult thought in a particular instance, though it may be; it means only that the potential has been achieved.

Assimilation and accommodation, prompted by disequilibrium, continue throughout life to produce changes in schemata. After the development of formal operations, changes in reasoning abilitites are quantitative and no longer qualitative with respect to logical operations and structure. The quality of reasoning one is capable of does not improve after this stage. The content and function of intelligence may improve. This does not mean that the use of thought cannot or does not improve after adolescence. The content and function of thought are free to vary and improve after this stage, which in part helps explain some of the classical differences between adolescent thought and adult thought.

One should not assume that all adolescents and adults fully develop formal operations. Several studies concluded that no more than half the American population develops all the possibilities of formal operations (Elkind 1962; Kohlberg and Mayer 1972; Schwebel 1975; and Kuhn et al. 1977). Certainly a proportion of the American adult population never advances much beyond concrete operational reasoning.

HOW FORMAL OPERATIONS DIFFER FROM CONCRETE OPERATIONS

Functionally, formal thought and concrete thought are similar. They both employ logical operations. The major difference between the two kinds of thought is the much greater range of application and type of logical operations available to the child with formal thought. Concrete thought is limited to solving tangible concrete problems known in the present. Concrete operational children cannot deal with complex verbal problems involving propositions, hypothetical problems, or those involving the future. The reasoning of concrete operational children is "content bound"— tied to available experience. To this extent, a concrete operational child is not completely free of past and present perceptions. In contrast, a child with fully developed formal operations can deal with all classes of problems, as well as with the present, past, and future, the hypothetical, and verbal propositional problems. During this stage the child becomes capable of introspection and is able to think about his or her own thoughts and feelings as if they were objects. Thus the child with formal operations is capable of reasoning in a manner that is more fully independent of past and current experiences. Reasoning becomes increasingly capable of being "content free" during this stage.

A concrete operational child must deal with each problem in isolation; reasoning operations are not coordinated. The child cannot integrate his or her solutions by means of general theories. A child with formal operations has the capability to employ theories and hypotheses in the solution of problems. Several intellectual operations can be brought to bear simultaneously and systematically on a problem.

In addition, formal operations are characterized by scientific reasoning and hypothesis building (and testing), and they reflect a highly developed understanding of causation. For the first time, the child can operate on the logic of an argument (problem) independent of its content. He or she is aware that logically derived conclusions have a validity independent of factual truth. While concrete thought and formal thought are both logical, they are clearly different. The concrete operational child lacks the range, power, and depth of reasoning of his or her more developed counterpart.

Formal cognitive thought and reasoning arise out of concrete operations in the same way that each new level of thought incorporates and modifies prior thought. Formal thought has the structural properties of being hypothetical-deductive, scientific-inductive, and reflexive-abstractive. In addition, formal thought operates on *contents* that Piaget called *propositional*, or *combinatorial*, and *formal operational schemes.* These structural properties and contents are illustrated in this chapter by a series of problems from Piaget's work. The examples are taken primarily from Piaget and Inhelder 1958 and Piaget 1972a, the two most important works by Piaget on cognitive development during the adolescent years.

STRUCTURES DEVELOPED IN THE FORMAL OPERATIONAL STAGE

Hypothetical-Deductive Reasoning

Hypothetical reasoning "goes beyond the confines of everyday experience to things which we have no experience" (Brainerd 1978, p. 205). It is reasoning that transcends perception and memory and deals with things we have not directly known, things that are hypothetical.

Deductive reasoning is reasoning from premises to conclusion or from the general to the specific. Inferences or conclusions based on deductive reasoning are necessarily true only if the premises they are derived from are true. Reasoning can be applied to arguments that have false premises, however, and logical conclusions can be derived.

Hypothetical-deductive reasoning is reasoning that "involves deducing conclusions from premises which are *hypotheses* rather than from facts that the subject has actually verified" (ibid.). In this manner the possible (hypothetical) becomes an arena within which reasoning can be used effectively.

Children with formal operations can reason about hypothetical problems entirely symbolically (in their minds) and can deduce logical conclusions. Thus, when they are presented with a problem in a form "A is less than B, and B is less than C; is A less than C?" they can reason appropriately from the premise ($A < B$ and $B < C$) and deduce that A is less than C ($A < C$). When given the verbal problem "Bob is left of Sam, and Sam is left of Bill; is Bob left of Bill?" those with formal operations can make the correct deduction from the hypothesis or premises. Concrete operational children cannot solve problems in this form.

Another feature of hypothetical-deductive reasoning during formal operations is the ability to reason about hypotheses believed to be untrue (false premises) and still come to logical conclusions that can be inferred from the hypotheses. If a logical argument is prefixed by the statement "Suppose coal is white," the concrete operational child, when asked to solve the logical problem, declares that coal is black and that the question cannot be answered. The child with formal operations readily accepts the assumption that the coal is white and proceeds to reason about the logic of the argument. The older child can submit to logical analysis the *structure* of the argument, independent of the truth or falseness of its content.

Scientific-Inductive Reasoning

Inductive reasoning is reasoning from specific facts to general conclusions. It is the main reasoning process used by scientists to arrive at generalizations or scientific laws.

Inhelder and Piaget (1958) concluded that when confronted with problems, children with formal operations are capable of reasoning very much like scientists. They form hypotheses, experiment, control variables, record effects, and from their results draw conclusions in a systematic manner. Two examples from this work are presented in this section to illustrate scientific-inductive reasoning in formal thought.

One of the characteristics of scientific reasoning is the ability to think about a number of different variables at the same time. Those with formal reasoning accomplish this in a coordinated manner and can determine the effect of one, all, or some combination of a set of variables. Piaget referred to this as *combinatorial reasoning*. Combinatorial reasoning, or reasoning about a number of variables at one time, is not something that a concrete operational child can do. Concrete operational children typically can reason successfully only when there is a single variable or when causes can be determined directly from observation. Formal reasoning goes beyond observation.

The Colorless Chemical Liquid Problem. In the colorless chemical liquid problem, a child is presented with five glasses or jars, each containing a different colorless liquid (see Figure 6.1). Four of the five containers look exactly the same. The fifth container contains an eyedropper as well as a clear liquid (potassium iodide, labeled g). Water oxidizes potassium iodide in an acid mixture, turning the mixture yellow. Water (2) is neutral, and thiosulphate (4) is a bleach. The child is given two glasses, one containing water (2) and the other containing sulphuric acid and oxygenated water (1 + 3). The experimenter puts several drops of potassium iodide (g) in each of the two glasses, and reactions are noted. The child is asked to reproduce the yellow color by using the five original containers in any way that

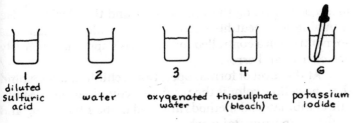

FIGURE 6.1

he wishes. If the yellow color is produced, the child is asked to explain how this was accomplished. The only combinations that will produce the yellow color are $1 + 3 + g$ or $1 + 3 + g + 2$; the former is the simpler solution. There are 25 possible combinations of two or more of the liquids. The solution to the problem cannot be determined from observation alone.

At the preoperational level, children do little more than try different combinations of two liquids at a time in an unsystematic manner. At the concrete operational level, efforts are more systematic but not fully so. Combinations of three and four liquids are frequently tried, but concrete methods are primarily trial and error. Occasionally these methods produce the yellow-colored combination, but concrete operational children cannot repeat the process nor explain how they got it.

> Kis (9;6) begins with $(3 \times g) + (1 \times g) + (2 \times g) + (4 \times g)$, after which he spontaneously mixes the contents of the four glasses in another glass; but there are no further results. "O.K., we start over again." This time he mixes $4 \times g$ first, then $1 \times g$: "No result." Then he adds $2 \times g$, looks and finally puts in $3 \times g$. "Another try ($1 \times g$, then $2 \times g$, then $3 \times g$). Ah! (yellow appeared, but he added $4 \times g$). Oh! So that! So that's (4) what takes away the color. 3 gives the best color." "Can you make the color with fewer bottles?"— "No."—"Try" (He undertakes several 2 by 2 combinations, but at random.) (Ibid.)

Kis, who is concrete operational, tries different two-by-two combinations. He mixes different combinations and succeeds in getting the yellow color and then losing it. He is unable to repeat his success. All possible combinations are not tried in a controlled manner. Kis's approach is largely one of trial and error.

At the level of formal operations, children understand that the yellow color is the result of a combination. Systematic combinatorial methods are used in their reasoning and in their experimental work.

> Sar (12;3) . . . *"I'd better write it down to remind myself: 1 x 4 is done; 4 × 3 is done; and 2 x 3. Several more that I haven't done* (he finds all six, then adds the drops and find yellow from 1 x 3 x g). *Ah! it's turning yellow. You need 1, 3, and the drops."*— "Where is the yellow?" . . . *"In there?"* (g)—"No, they go together."—"And 2?"—*"I don't think it has any effect, it's water."*—"And 4?"—*"It doesn't do anything either, it's water too. But I want to try again; you can't ever be too sure.* . . . (he puts together 1 x 3 x 2 x g, then 1 x 3 x 4 x g) *Ah! There it is! That one* (4) *keeps it from coloring."*—"And that?" (2).—*"It's water."*
> (Ibid., pp. 116-17)

Sar quickly realizes that a systematic combinatorial approach is called for, and he proceeds to sort out the combinations of variables. Each combination is tested for the effect. For children with formal operations, combinatorial reasoning is an instrument for conclusive deduction. The solution to this kind of problem cannot be derived from observation alone.

The Pendulum Problem.   In the colorless liquid problem, children had to search out the set of variables that would produce an effect. The pendulum problem (Figure 6.2) also requires combinatorial reasoning, but to a different end. Solving the pendulum problem requires one to *exclude* rather than include variables.

A weight suspended on the end of a piece of string and then set in motion acts as a pendulum. Children provided with strings of varying lengths and different weights are asked to determine and explain what controls the pendu-

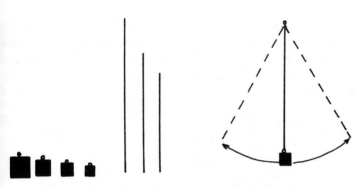

FIGURE 6.2

lum's rate of movement and oscillation. The factors usually considered by children are the length of the string, the weight at the end of the string, the height from which the weight is dropped to start the motion, and the force or push in starting the pendulum in motion.

The single factor that controls the rate of oscillation or movement of the pendulum is the length of the string. Thus, ". . . the problem is to isolate it (length of the string) from the other three and to exclude them. Only in this way can the subject explain and vary the frequency of oscillations and solve the problem" (ibid., p. 69).

At the preoperational level, most children believe that the pendulum's rate of movement is dependent on their push of it.

> One can see . . . that because of the lack of serial ordering and exact correspondences the subject cannot either give an objective account of the experiment or even give consistent explanations which are not mutually contradictory. It is especially obvious that the child constantly interferes with the pendulum's motion without being able to dissociate the impetus which he gives it from the motion which is independent of his action. (Ibid.)

At the level of concrete operations, children typically discover the relation between the length of the pendulum's string and its rate of movement. Even so, they are unable to separate the variables and attribute the movement exclusively to the length of the string. They are convinced that weight and "push" have something to do with the oscillation.

> Jac (8;0) after several trials in which he has varied the length of the string: *"The less high it is* (the shorter the string), *the faster it goes."* The suspended weight, on the other hand, gives rise to incoherent relationships: *"With the big ones* (the heavy ones) *it falls better, it goes faster,* for example, *It's not that one* (500 grams), *it's this one* (100 grams) *that goes slower."* But after a new trial, he says in reference to the 100-gram weight: *"It goes faster"*—"What do you have to do for it to go faster?"—*"Put on two weights."*—"Or else?"—*"Don't put on any: it goes faster when it's lighter."* As for the dropping point. *"If you let go very low down, it goes very fast,"* and *"It goes faster if you let go high up,"* but in the second case Jac has also shortened the string. (Ibid., p. 70)

Typical concrete operational children are able to correctly *order* the effects of altering one variable (the length of string). They are unable to conclude that one factor alone controls the rate of movement of the pendulum. They cannot *exclude* from causality the other factors. According to Inhelder and Piaget, children at the level of formal operations "are able to isolate all of the variables present by varying a single factor while holding all the other things equal" (ibid., p. 75).

> Eme (15;1) after having selected 100 grams with a long string and medium length string, the 20 grams with a long and short string, and finally 200 grams with a long and short, concludes: "It's the length of the string that makes it go faster or slower; the weight doesn't play any role." She discounts likewise the height of the drop and the force of the push. (Ibid.)

The older child's experimentation and reasoning are systematic. One variable or factor is altered at a time, while all others remain constant. All possibilities are explored. The child with formal operations can apply combinatorial reasoning and can exclude variables that do not have any effect.

It is interesting to note that the two problems just presented are "concrete" problems. Concrete operational children cannot reason successfully about these problems, though they can reason successfully about other concrete problems, such as most conservation problems. Though both kinds of problems are concrete problems, the colorless liquid problem and the pendulum problem require more than observation in order to be solved. In most conservation problems (those discussed earlier) all the necessary information needed to solve the problems is supplied and observable by the child. Either reversibility by inversion or reciprocity is sufficient to ensure understanding. In the colorless liquid problem and the pendulum problem all the relevant information *is not* given. In each case the relationships between the variables must be *constructed* through inductive (scientific) reasoning and verified by experimentation. Reversibility and concrete thought alone do not permit the concrete operational child to do this.

Reflective Abstraction

Reflective abstraction is one of the mechanisms by which cognitive construction takes place. In our earlier discussion of knowledge, physical knowledge and logical-mathematical knowledge were differentiated. Physical knowledge is knowledge of the physical properties of objects derived by the manipulation of objects. Logical-mathematical knowledge is knowledge constructed from physical or mental *actions* on objects. The mechanisms through which physical and logical-mathematical knowledge are derived are called empirical abstraction and reflective abstraction.

Reflective abstraction (as in the construction of logical-mathematical knowledge) always goes beyond the observable and results in mental reorganization. Reflective abstraction always involves an abstraction from a lower level to a higher level. The major mechanism present in the construction of all logical-mathematical knowledge is reflective abstraction.

Reflective abstraction is internal thought or reflection based on available knowledge. At the formal operational level, internal reflection can result in new knowledge—new construction. Concrete operational children cannot construct new knowledge from internal reflection alone (Brainerd 1978).

Analogies.   In a study of reflective abstraction published in 1977, Piaget examined children's understanding of analogies (Gallagher and Reid 1981). Analogies are of interest because they require a construction of *relationships* between the members that comprise the analogy. According to Piaget, these relationships can come about only through reflective abstraction. The relationships in analogies cannot be deduced directly from experience. For example, consider this analogy: Dog is to hair as bird is to feathers. The four members of the analogy—dog, bird, hair, and feathers—are all common objects known to most people through experience. The heart of the analogy is the relationship between dog-hair and bird-feathers. The relationship is not observable and comes about through reflection (reflective abstraction).

Children between age 5 and age 13 were asked to pair and arrange in a two-by-two matrix the pictures in Figure 6.3. A child who had difficulty establishing pairs or arranging the pairs in a matrix was asked questions such as, "What does a vacuum cleaner run on?" "What does a car run on?" All children were asked for the reasons why they thought particular items went together.

When analogical sets were established correctly in a matrix, countersuggestions were provided, such as, "Does the rug (E) go as well here as the electric outlet (D)?" Countersuggestions were used to determine whether the child was reasoning with analogy and how resistant to suggestion this reasoning was.

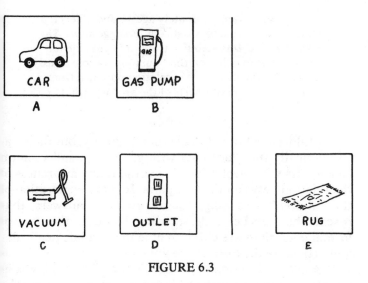

FIGURE 6.3

Gallagher and Read report that Piaget's research led to the identification of three distinct levels of understanding and reasoning about analogies.

> The younger children at stage 1 (ages 5 and 6) were more likely to arrange pairs but ignore the complete analogical form. For example, they stated that the dog needs hair to keep warm and the bird needs feathers to fly. The relationship between dog and hair (*A* is to *B*) was not compared to the relationship between bird and feathers (*C* is to *D*). For Piaget this is an example of empirical abstraction—attending to the observable characteristics—which prevents true solution according to the analogical form of *A:B* as *C:D*. . . .
>
> Children at stage 2 (approximately ages 8 to 11) were able to complete the matrices. But when countersuggestions were made, the analogical form proved to be weak and the answers were changed. However, according to Piaget, the ability to complete the matrices demonstrated reflexive abstraction—the projection to a higher level of that which is drawn from a lower level. . . .

At stage 3 (approximately age 11 and older) the children were able to resist countersuggestions. The form *A:B* as *C:D* is stabilized, and it is possible for the subjects to *reflect* on their answers by consciously explaining the hierarchical relation obtained from consideration of both parts of the analogy. (Ibid., pp. 117–118)

Children in Stage 1 may group correctly, but they reason typically that "auto fits with gas pump, and vacuum cleaner fits with electric outlet" without any awareness of the relation between the two pairs. It is the exploration of the children's *reasoning*, not merely their answers, that reveals their level of understanding. Not until the stage of formal operations are children able to use analogical rules and articulate the form of the analogy.

Analogical reasoning is an example of reasoning constructed almost exclusively independent of content. The central characteristic of analogy is the relation between the pairs. This clearly goes beyond what is observable.

CONTENT OF FORMAL THOUGHT

I have noted the primary structural characteristics of formal thought that differentiate it from concrete thought. About what kind of *contents*, then, are those with formal operations able to reason, and those with concrete operations not able to reason? Piaget identified the contents of formal thought as *propositional operations* and *formal operational schemes*.

Propositional, or Combinatorial, Operations

Inhelder and Piaget (1958) set forth Piaget's belief that reasoning during the stage of formal operations is similar in many respects to the propositional logic used by logicians. Such thought is logical, abstract, and systematic. An understanding of symbolic logic is required to fully appreciate Piaget's perspective.

I will leave the task of explaining propositional logic and the details of Piaget's view to others (see Brainerd 1981; Ginsburg and Opper 1979) and instead look at the kind of reasoning used by formal operational children that bears a resemblance to propositional logic.

One task used by Piaget and Inhelder to examine the use of propositional reasoning was the pendulum problem described earlier in this chapter. I suggested that it was only at the level of formal operations that children reason systematically about the causes of the pendulum's oscillation. They go through several steps including generating hypotheses, designing and carrying out experiments, observing results, and drawing conclusions from their results.

In the pendulum problem, the factors of length of the pendulum string, the pendulum's weight, height of release, and push at release could all be hypothesized, either alone or in combination, as responsible for the oscillation.

The design of an experiment typically takes two of these factors and combines them in all possible combinations. Length of string and weight of pendulum could be tried in four possible combinations, and the rate of oscillation observed for each combination. Table 6.1 shows these four combinations and the observed (1–4) and not observed results (5–8) on oscillation.

Looking at the results regarding the weight factor, it is clear that there is no relation between weight and oscillation. Both heavy weights and light weights have slow and fast oscillations. Weight by itself can thus be eliminated as a causal factor. Looking at the results for length of the pendulum string, one observes a consistent pattern. When the string is long, regardless of the weight, the oscillation of the pendulum is *always* slow. When the string is short, the oscillation is *always* fast. It is clear that the length of the pendulum string *does* play a role in determining the rate of oscillation and that the weight of the pendulum does *not* play a role. Length of pendulum implies oscillation; weight of pendulum does not.

Table 6.1
The Pendulum Problem:
Four Combinations

	Factors		Results
	Length	*Weight*	*Oscillation*
1.	long	light	slow[a]
2.	short	light	fast[a]
3.	long	heavy	slow[a]
4.	short	heavy	fast[a]
5.	long	light	fast[b]
6.	short	light	slow[b]
7.	long	heavy	fast[b]
8.	short	heavy	slow[b]

[a]Results observed.
[b]Results not observed.

The above experiment combined two of the four factors in all four possible combinations. Similar experiments can be carried out to determine the roles, if any, of the other two factors, height of release and push of pendulum, in combination with each other, and each in the various possible combinations of the other three. Children with formal operations do not always structure their investigations or experiments as formally as suggested in Table 6.1, but they are capable of using the kind of reasoning shown. Combinatorial procedures like these permit adolescents with formal operations to arrive at conclusions that are certain.[1]

Formal Operational Schemes

Formal operational schemes are less "abstract" than propositional schemes and bear a closer likeness to scientific reasoning than propositional operations do. Two examples of formal operational schemes, *proportion* and *probability*, are examined next.

The development of children's concepts of proportion can be seen in their actions with a seesaw balance, such as the one shown in Figure 6.4. Before age 7, children have difficulty equalizing weights on a balance. They are aware that a balance is possible, but their attempts to attain it are always successive trial-and-error corrections. Compensation on the balance is never systematic. After age 7 (the age of concrete operations), children discover that a small weight placed farther from the fulcrum can balance a larger weight placed closer to it. They learn to equalize weight and length in a systematic manner. But they do not coordinate the two functions of weight and length as a proportion.

Around age 13, comprehension of the proportion principle ($W/L = 2W/2L$) occurs when the child becomes aware that an increase in weight on one side of the fulcrum can be compensated by an increase in distance from the fulcrum on the other side (Inhelder and Piaget 1958). Thus the development of a child's conception of proportion is consistent with his or her general conceptual development. Qualitative differences in schemata of proportion are found at different stages.

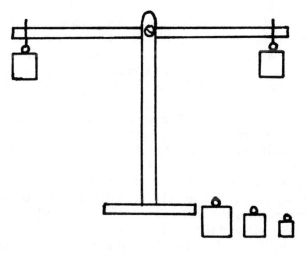

FIGURE 6.4

Probability

Probability is a concept based on understanding chance and proportion. Probability is not constructed before the stage of formal operations.

> ... the child must be capable of at least two operations characteristic of this level. He must be able to apply a combinatorial system that enables him to take into consideration all the possible combinations of the given elements; and he must be able to calculate proportions, however elementary, so that he can grasp the fact (which eludes subjects on the previous levels) that probabilities like 3/9 and 2/6, etc., are equivalent. It is not until the age of eleven or twelve that the child understands combinatorial probabilities. (Piaget and Inhelder 1969, p. 144)

Children's development of the probability concept can be assessed with the following procedure: A set of 96 one-inch wooden blocks of four different colors is placed on a table where they can be seen by the child. The distribution of the blocks by color is 36, 36, 20, and 4. The blocks are separated into groups by color, then each group is halved. Half the blocks of each color (18, 18, 10, 2) are set to one side as a reference set. The remaining blocks, which the child must acknowledge as identical to the reference set, are placed in a bag or box and hidden from view (see Figure 6.5).

The blocks in the bag are mixed up. The child is told that the examiner is going to pull 2 blocks from the bag without looking into the bag. The child is asked to predict what colors the 2 blocks will be. When the child responds, he or she is asked to explain the response. The blocks are drawn from the bag and placed on the table. The draws are repeated until the examiner *is sure* of the child's level of understanding of this kind of probability.

Until age 11 or 12, children generally make predictions on some basis other than probability, or with limited conviction in probability. Preoperational children rarely use

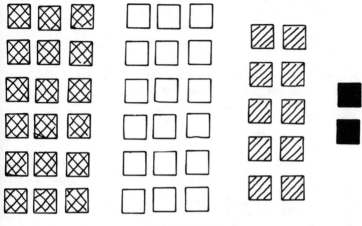

FIGURE 6.5

a strategy based on reasoning. They frequently predict the next colors to be drawn as the same as the previous blocks drawn, or they predict their favorite color. Most frequently, they just "guess." Concrete operational children frequently use a strategy, although they do not adhere to a probability strategy.

Children with formal operations typically respond to this kind of problem with responses based on probability. Their responses are always determined by the number of blocks of each color remaining in the bag. Research by Heard and Wadsworth (1977) found children understanding this problem, on the average, at age 12.

The concepts of proportion and probability developed during the stage of formal operations are examples of formal operational schemes. Such schemes are less abstract than propositional schemes because their functioning does not rely on deduction to the extent that propositional operations do.

AFFECTIVE DEVELOPMENT AND ADOLESCENCE

The development of affect during the stage of formal operations flows from the same source as the development of cognitive and intellectual structures. As we have seen throughout the course of development, intellectual development and affective development bear a common stamp.

During adolescence, affective development is characterized by two major factors: the development of *idealistic feelings* and the formation of the *personality*.

Idealistic Feelings

With the development of formal operations comes the emergence of abilities to reason about, and to think about, the hypothetical—the future—and to reflect on one's own thinking—to think about thinking. "Henceforth intelligence will be able to operate not only on objects and situations but also on hypotheses and, therefore, on the possible as well as the real" (Piaget 1981, p. 69).

If motivated to do so, children with formal reasoning can reason as logically as adults. The tools for an evaluation of intellectual arguments are formed and fully functional. One of the major affective differences between the thought of the adolescent and that of the adult is that initially in their use of formal operations, adolescents apply a criterion of pure logic in evaluating reasoning about human events. Adolescents lack a full appreciation of the way in which the world is ordered. With the capability for generating endless hypotheses, an adolescent also believes that what is best is what is logical. He or she does not yet differentiate between the logical world and the "real" world. The significance of adolescent idealistic feelings for adolescent behavior are explored later in this chapter in the discussion of adolescent egocentrism.

The Formation of Personality

The second major characteristic of affective development during adolescence is the formation of personality. During the adolescent years, while formal operations are developing, children begin to have their own feelings or views about people. "Up until 12 or so, feelings are of a concrete sort directed towards objects or towards other people. Such values as [the child] places on ideas are often other people's values" (ibid., p. 70).

These feelings and views are *autonomous* views that have their origins in the development of autonomy during the concrete operational stage. Many of these feelings are idealistic—at least in appearance. During this time, children come to have *their own* ideas about ideas.

> Personality formation begins in middle to late childhood (eight to twelve years) with the autonomous organization of rules and values, and the affirmation of will with respect to the regulation and hierarchical organization of moral tendencies.
> (Piaget 1967, p. 65)

Piaget distinguished between the personality and the self. The two can be seen as oriented in opposite directions. The self is oriented toward the individual. The self "is activity that is centered on the self" (Piaget 1981, p. 71). The personality is oriented toward the social world.

The self begins to develop in the first years of life. Personality, according to Piaget, does not begin to develop until the transition to adult life in adolescence. This necessarily involves a "subordination of the *self* to the collective ideal" (ibid.). The motive or adaptive power for personality to develop then, is the "desire" to fit into the world of work and adult life. Personality is "a matter of the fusion of one's work with one's individuality" (ibid.).

Personality formation grows out of the autonomous organization of rules and values at the concrete operational stage. As the adolescent unconsciously seeks to *adapt* to society and eventually to the world of real work, there is a submission of the *self* to some form of discipline.

> Personality implies cooperation and personal autonomy. It is opposed both to . . . the complete absence of rules, and to complete heteronomy, abject submission to the constraints imposed from without." (Piaget 1967, p. 65)

Personality, then, is the result of the autonomous individual's efforts to adapt to the social world of adulthood.

Moral Development during Adolescence

The development of moral reasoning begins in the sensori-motor stage and reaches its highest levels when formal operations and affective development are fully developed. In this section I discuss the development during adolescence of the moral concepts rules, lying, and justice.

Rules, Stage 4: Codification of Rules. Around the beginning of formal operations, at age 11 or 12, most children construct a relatively sophisticated understanding of rules. The rules of the game are seen as fixed at any point in time by mutual agreement and changeable through mutual agreement. The earlier belief that rules are permanent and externally imposed by an authority is no longer present. At this stage, the rules in use are known to all, and all agree on what the rules are. Adolescents recognize fully that rules are necessary for cooperation and to play the game effectively. There also seems to be an interest in rules for their own sake.

Lying. We have seen that preoperational children generally view a lie as something "naughty." Errors that are involuntary are still considered lies. Transgressions that do not result in punishment are not viewed as lies. Between age 7 and age 10, the criterion for whether a statement is a lie or not is whether the statement is true or false. All false statements are considered lies.

After age 10 or 11, children typically begin to recognize *in their reasoning* the role of intentions in lying and what constitutes a lie. At this level of reasoning, a lie is defined as something that is *intentionally* false. A full appreciation of intentions in moral judgments begins to develop around the transition from concrete to formal operations.

It was noted earlier that through age 7 or so, children view the avoidance of punishment as the reason for not lying. Indeed, the young child typically views a nonpunished act as necessarily not a lie. After age 9 or so, there is a separation of the concept of lie from punishment. The concrete operational child typically believes that a lie is wrong even if it goes unpunished.

Piaget observed that a maturing of children's concepts about lying generally occurs between age 10 and age 12. Intentions become the major criterion used to evaluate lying. The older child (with formal operations) also recognizes that *not lying* is necessary for cooperation. This is all part of a long shift from a morality of constraint to a morality of cooperation.

> In the first place a lie is wrong because it is
> an object of punishment; if the punishment were
> removed, it would be allowed. Then a lie becomes
> something that is wrong in itself and would remain
> so even if the punishment were removed. Finally, a
> lie is wrong because it is in conflict with mutual
> trust and affection. Thus the consciousness of lying
> gradually becomes interiorized and the hypothesis
> may be hazarded that it does so under the influence
> of cooperation. (Piaget 1965, p. 171)

Justice. Piaget suggested that the concept of "just punishment" begins to be constructed by children only after a comprehension of rules emerges, generally around age 7 or 8. Concepts of rules are developed as children interact with other children. All this is concurrent with a decline in intellectual egocentrism and an increased ability to see the viewpoint of others. In moral judgment we see an evolution from asocial judgments (expiatory punishment) to social judgments (reciprocity).

> ... in every domain we have studied up till now,
> respect for the adult—or at any rate a certain way of
> respecting the adult—diminishes in favor of the rela-
> tions of equality and reciprocity between children
> ... it is perfectly normal that in the domain of retri-
> bution [punishment] the effects of unilateral respect
> [egocentrism] should tend to diminish with age. . . .

Table 6.2

Relationship between Children's Cognitive Development and the Development of Concepts of Rules, Accidents, Lying, and Justice

Cognitive Development	Rules	Accidents	Lying	Justice
Sensori-motor (0–2 years)	Motor stage. Rules not observed			
Preoperational (2–7 years)	Egocentric stage. Games played in isolation; no cooperation or social interaction	Intentions not considered. Children do not take the view of others. Judgments based on quantitative effects of actions	Punishment the criterion for lie. No punishment = no lie. Lying is like being "naughty"	Submission to adult authority. Arbitrary, expiatory punishments considered just
Concrete operations (7–11 years)	Incipient cooperation. Rules observed, though little agreement as to what the rules are	Intentions begin to be considered. Children begin to take the view of	Lie = not true. Unpunished untruths are lies	Justice based on reciprocity. Equality more important than authority

Formal operations (after 11–12 years)	Codification of rules. Rules known to all; agreement as to what the rules are; rules can be changed by consensus; rules of interest for their own sake	Intentions decide whether a false statement is not a lie. Truthfulness viewed as necessary for cooperation	Equality with equity. Reciprocity considers intent and circumstances

What remains of the idea of retribution is the notion, not that one must compensate for the offence by a proportional suffering, but that one must make the offender realize, by means of measures appropriate to the fault itself, in what way he has broken the bond of solidarity. . . .

the idea of reciprocity, often taken at first as a sort of legalized vengeance or law of retaliation . . . tends of itself towards a morality of forgiveness and understanding . . . the time comes when the child realizes that there can be reciprocity only in well-doing. . . . The law of reciprocity implies certain positive obligations in virtue of its very form. And this is why the child, once he has admitted the principle of punishment by reciprocity in the sphere of justice, often comes to feel that any punitive element is unnecessary, even if it is "motivated," the essential thing being to make the offender realize that his action was wrong, in so far as it was contrary to the rules of cooperation. (Piaget 1965, p. 232)

Piaget concluded that three major periods exist in the development of children's concepts of justice. The first period lasts until age 7 or 8. In this period, justice is subordinated to adult authority. The child accepts as "just" whatever adults (authorities) say is right. There is no distinction between the notion of just and unjust and the notion of duty and disobedience (Gruber and Voheche 1977, p. 187). The child considers punishment to be the essence of justice.

The second period, between age 8 and age 11, evolves around concepts of cooperation. Reciprocity is viewed as the appropriate basis for punishment. A major emphasis is placed on "equality" of punishment, that laws are interpreted equally for all and that all should receive the same (equal) punishment for the same "crime" regardless of the circumstance. Equality is viewed as more important than punishment. Expiatory punishment is no longer viewed as "just."

In the third period, usually beginning around age 11 or 12, reciprocity remains the basis for children's judgments about punishment, but children now consider intentions and situational variables (extenuating circumstances) when formulating judgments. Piaget called this *equity*. Punishment need no longer be dispensed "equally" in a quantitative sense. For example, young children are held less liable than older children. At this level of development, judgments based on equity may be considered by the reader to be a more effective implementation of equality.

COGNITIVE DEVELOPMENT AND ADOLESCENCE

Adolescent behavior has always been a matter of concern to parents, educators, and psychologists.[2] Many theorists since G. Stanley Hall (1908) have tried to account for the unique characteristics of the adolescent period. Psychoanalytic theory (Freud 1946; Erickson 1959) offers a rationale for affective and social aspects of adolescent behavior, though there has been little supporting research for this position. Behaviorists, by and large, have avoided the topic of adolescence. While adolescence has received considerable attention in educational and psychological literature, little of this attention has been concerned with the intellectual development of the older child and the possible effects of the unique characteristics of adolescent reasoning on adolescent behavior.

Piaget recognized the roles that maturation and sexual awareness play during the adolescent years, but he suggested that these facts are inadequate to explain adolescence.

> But these well known facts, made banal by certain psychological writings, far from exhaust the analysis of adolescence. Indeed, pubertal changes would play only a very secondary role if the thinking and emotions characteristic of adolescence were accorded their true significance. (Piaget 1967, p. 60)

One characteristic of adolescents is their ability to "catch" adults using illogical reasoning. Every teacher and parent has experienced this persistent and sometimes frustrating characteristic, which is not found in younger children. It occurs in children with formal operations because they have developed reasoning and logical abilities that are in some ways *equal* to those of adults. Like adults with formal reasoning, adolescents with formal reasoning do not always use it, but once the reasoning is developed, adolescents have the same capabilities for reasoning as adults do.

A major difference between adult and adolescent reasoning capabilities is the sheer *number of schemata*, or structures. The development of new schemata or new areas of knowledge does not stop with the attainment of formal operations. As people continue to have new experiences, they continue to develop new schemata and concepts. The adult's range of experiences typically is much greater than the adolescent's. Thus, the typical adult possesses more structures, or "content," to which he or she can apply reasoning powers than does the typical adolescent.

The aspect of Piaget's work that has probably been most neglected is that which attempts to account for the uniqueness of adolescent thought and behavior. While Piaget did not attempt to explain all adolescent behavior, he did provide an important link between cognitive development, affective development, and general behavior. It is unfortunate that Piaget's thoughts on this topic have not attracted more interest and attention, particularly among parents and teachers of adolescents.

Piaget's explanation of adolescent behavior is consistent with the rest of his theory. He saw the unique characteristics of adolescent thought and personality as a normal outgrowth of development. That is, much of adolescent thought and behavior can be explained by prior development. In this respect, the development of cognitive structures before and during adolescence helps account for the characteristics of behavior during the period.

The adolescent is typically one who has entered the stage of formal operations and is developing, or has developed, the cognitive skills and affective reasoning characteristic of that stage. Logical operations permit the child to reason logically about a wide range of logical problems. At this point, the qualitative development of cognitive structures is presumed complete. The typical adolescent has the mental apparatus required to solve problems logically as well as adults can. Why, then, does the adolescent "think differently" from the adult?

Piaget believed that the characteristics of adolescent thought that make the adolescent unique are in part due to the child's level of cognitive development and his or her accompanying *egocentrism* of thought.

Egocentrism and Adolescence

Egocentrism is a constant companion of cognitive development. At each new stage of mental growth, a child's inability to differentiate assumes a different form and is expressed in a novel set of behaviors. Thus one of the characteristics of thought associated with *all* newly acquired cognitive structures is egocentrism. This is a by-product of mental development that, in a sense, distorts the initial use of newly acquired cognitive structures. Each period of development finds egocentrism manifest in a unique form.

During the sensori-motor period (0–2 years), a child is egocentric in the sense that he (or she) cannot differentiate between other objects and himself as an object, nor between objects and his sensory impressions. He is the center of his world. With development during the period, this egocentrism subsides. By the time the child becomes able to internally represent objects and events, this form of egocentrism is diminished. The egocentrism of the preoperational period (2–7 years) is seen in the inability of children to differentiate between their thoughts and those of others. They believe their thoughts are always correct. As social interaction with others (particularly peers) increases, this form of egocentrism subsides. Elkind suggests that the preoperational child is also egocentric in being unable to differentiate between symbols (words) and their referents. The child in this stage is seen to give incomplete verbal descriptions to others, believing that words carry more information than they really do (Elkind 1967, p. 1025).

During concrete operations (7–11 years), a child becomes able to apply logical operations to concrete problems. Egocentrism takes the form of inability to differentiate between perceptual events and mental constructions. The child cannot "think" independently of her (or his) perceptions. She is not aware of what are thoughts and what are perceptions. Hypotheses requiring perceptually untrue assumptions ("coal is white") cannot be pursued. With the attainment of formal operations and the ability to reflect on one's own thought, this form of egocentrism diminishes.

As each new plane of cognitive functioning is initially characterized by a form of egocentrism, so too are formal operations and adolescence. The adolescent, in a sense, is possessed by his or her new-found powers of logical thought. In adolescent thought, the criterion for making judgments becomes what is logical to the adolescent, as if what is logical in the eyes of the adolescent is *always* right, and what is illogical is *always* wrong. The egocentrism of adolescence is the inability to differentiate between the adolescent's world and the "real" world. The adolescent is emboldened with an egocentric belief in the omnipotence of logical thought. Because the adolescent boy can think logically about the future and about hypothetical people and events, he feels that the world should submit itself to logical schemes rather than to systems of reality. He does not understand that the world is not always logically or rationally ordered, as he thinks it should be.

> . . . when the cognitive field is again enlarged by the structuring of formal thought, a . . . form of egocentrism comes into view. This egocentrism is one of the most enduring features of adolescence . . . the adolescent not only tries to adapt his ego to the social environment but, just as emphatically, tries to adjust the environment to his ego. . . . The result is a relative failure to distinguish between his point of view . . . and the point of view of the group which he hopes to reform. . . . But we believe that, in the egocentrism found in the adolescent, there is more than a simple desire to deviate; rather, it is a manifestation of the phenomenon of lack of differentiation . . . the adolescent goes through a phase in which he attributes an unlimited power to his own thoughts so

> that the dreams of a glorious future of transforming
> the world through ideas . . . seems to be not only fan-
> tasy but also an effective action which in itself modi-
> fies the empirical world. (Inhelder and Piaget, 1958,
> pp. 343–46)

To some extent the differences between the thought of adolescents and that of adults are a function of the normal course of cognitive development.

> We have seen that the principal intellectual
> characteristics of adolescence stem directly or indi-
> rectly from the development of formal structures.
> Thus, the latter is the most important event in the
> thinking found in this period. (Ibid., p. 347)

> The adolescent . . . thanks to his budding person-
> ality, sees himself as equal to elders, yet different
> from them . . . He wants to surpass and astound
> them by transforming the world. That is why the
> adolescent's systems or life plans are at the same
> time filled with generous sentiments and altruistic
> or mystically fervent projects and with disquieting
> megalomania and conscious egocentricity. (Piaget
> 1968, p. 66)

Adolescents are frequently involved in idealistic crises. They have the powers of formal reasoning but they cannot distinguish between the new powers and their application to real problems. It might seem that adolescents are doomed forever to be idealistic social critics. But as the egocentrism of other periods gradually diminished, so does the egocentrism of adolescence. Egocentrism subsides when the adolescent learns to use logic effectively in relation to the reality of life, and recognizes that all human and worldly events cannot be judged strictly against a criteria of what is logical.

> . . . the focal point of the decentering process is
> the entrance into the occupational world or the
> beginning of serious professional training. The ado-
> lescent becomes an adult when he undertakes a real

> job. It is then that he is transformed from an idealistic reformer into an achiever. In other words, the job leads thinking away from the dangers of formalism back into reality. (Inhelder and Piaget 1958, p. 346)

Thus, in Piaget's view, when (and if) adolescents attempt to become a part of the world of work and achievement, they are compelled to further *adapt* their reasoning and intelligence to the world as it is, rather than as they reason logically it should be.

Idealism

The reasoning of adolescents who have developed formal operations invariably seems to be idealistic. This *idealism* can be viewed as "false," or incomplete, idealism. What looks like idealism may in reality be reasoning based on an *egocentric* use of formal thought. When a typical adolescent with formal operations makes judgments based on reasoning, his or her conclusions seem to be idealistic because they are "logical." But the adolescent's logic and reasoning frequently do not take into account realities of human behavior that have nothing to do with logic.

Society confirms the biblical dictate "Thou shalt not kill," yet, historically, societies have sanctioned wars, the death penalty for certain crimes, and other "killings." From an adolescent's egocentric-logical point of view, these behaviors are illogical and thus wrong. The adolescent does not (cannot) take into account the many *real* causes of human and societal behaviors. Similarly, parents instruct their children not to smoke or drink, yet the parents engage in those activities themselves. To the adolescent this seems illogical. The adolescent may argue logically that if my parents (and peers) can smoke and drink, so can I.

The adolescent must learn to assume adult (realistic) roles in the real world. This involves not only cognitive development but also a parallel affective development. The dilemma of human behavior is more than a logical problem, and it is this perspective that adolescents typically do not appreciate until they have encountered reality in a *seri-*

ous way and have adapted to the "real" world. When the world is encountered as it really is, not merely as the adolescent thinks it should or could be, adaptations can be made that permit a shift from a logical-egocentric perspective to a logical-realistic perspective. With egocentrism adapted to reality, the capability for a realistic form of idealism occurs, an idealism that is able to appreciate the logical *and* nonlogical complexities of problems.

American society has greatly extended the length of time that adolescents and young adults spend in the period of *false idealism*. Many people do not begin a "real job" until after college graduation or even later. For them, the adaptation of logical reasoning to reality may be postponed.

The Reformer

One manifestation of adolescent egocentrism is seen in adolescents' desire to reform society. In their discussions about society, adolescents are frequently severe critics of society and its institutions. This behavior is frequently viewed by adults as antisocial, rebellious, unthoughtful, ungrateful, and generally wrong and inappropriate. Piaget argued that this is not always the case. In Piaget's view, the adolescent's desire to reform society can be attributed in large part to his or her intellectual capabilities for reasoning about the way things could be (hypothetically and logically), and to adolescent egocentrism.

> . . . the adolescent frequently appears asocial and practically asociable. Nothing, however, could be less true, since he is constantly meditating about society. The society that interests him is the society he wants to reform; he has nothing but disdain or disinterest for the real society he condemns. Furthermore, adolescent sociability develops through the young person's interaction with other adolescents. . . . Adolescents' social interaction . . . is aimed primarily at discussion. Whether in twosomes or in small coteries, the world is reconstructed in common, and the adolescent loses himself in endless dis-

cussion as a means of combating the real world.
(Piaget 1967, p. 68)

> We see, then, how the adolescent goes about
> injecting himself into adult society. He does so by
> means of projects, life plans, theoretical systems, and
> ideals of political or social reform. In short, he does
> so by means of thinking, and almost, one might say,
> by imagination—so far does this hypothetico-deduc-
> tive thinking sometimes depart from reality. (Ibid.,
> p. 67)

Piaget believed that, in part, adolescents' thought and
reasoning are necessarily those of a dreamer of better (more
logical) worlds. Some of this thought spills over into adolescent behavior, and we frequently see the adolescent in
the role of "reformer." Piaget made clear that such reasoning, though egocentric, is a natural and normal phase in
the development and refining of adolescent intelligence. The
reformer phase can be viewed as *necessary* for eventual
equilibration at a higher level.

What, then, moves the adolescent beyond the reformer
stage? What provides the disequilibrium necessary for further development?

> True adaptation to society comes automatically
> when the adolescent reformer attempts to put his
> ideas to work. Just as experience reconciles formal
> thought with the reality of things, so does effective
> and enduring work, undertaken in concrete and well-
> defined situations, cure all dreams. (Ibid., p. 69)

Thus, when adolescents attempt to implement their
theories, dreams, and hypotheses in the real world, the world
provides disequilibrium and provokes adjustments in
hypotheses. The striving to become an effective member of
society is part of the motivation that activates further
development.

The mental and affective developments of adolescence
are essential to the subsequent development of adult thought,
but they do not ensure realistic adult thought. The imple-

mentation of formal thought in adolescence is initially egocentric. The adolescent does not differentiate at first between
many possible perspectives. Adolescent thought initially is
idealistic-logical, and frequently it is manifest in criticism
of society and an elaboration of ideal worlds. Objectivity of
thought with respect to conflicting issues is attained and
egocentrism is diminished when the adolescent assumes an
adult role in the world and can differentiate the many possible points of view (Inhelder and Piaget 1958, p. 345).

SUMMARY

The stage of formal operations, which usually begins
around age 12 and is complete at age 16 or later, builds
upon, incorporates, and extends the development of concrete operations. Whereas concrete operational thought is
logical thought, it is restricted to the "concrete" world. Not
until the development of formal operations does reasoning
become "content free" or "concrete free." Formal reasoning
can deal with the *possible* as well as with the *real*.

Concrete operational thought is reversible thought.
Inversion and reciprocity are used independently, and the
two reversibilities become coordinated in formal thought.

Several *structures* emerge during the construction of
formal operations. *Hypothetical-deductive* reasoning is the
ability to reason about the hypothetical as well as the real
and the ability to deduce conclusions from hypothetical
premises. *Scientific-inductive* thought is reasoning from the
specific to the general; it is the kind of thought typical of
the scientist. Those with formal reasoning can explore all
possible relations in concrete or hypothetical problems.
Reflective abstraction is the abstraction of new knowledge
from existing knowledge gained by reflection or thought.
Reflective abstraction always goes beyond the observable
and is the primary mechanism of logical-mathematical
knowing.

Two major cognitive *contents* develop during formal
operations: *propositional*, or *combinatorial*, operations and
formal operational schemes. Propositional reasoning is sim-

ilar to propositional or symbolic logic in capability. It is abstract and systematic. Formal operational schemes, such as proportion and probability, bear a closer likeness to scientific reasoning. They are less abstract than propositional reasoning.

The cognitive capabilities of the adolescent with fully developed formal operations are qualitatitively equal to those of the adult. Adolescents can reason as logically as adults with formal operations can, although adults, by virtue of their greater experience, may be able to reason about more things than adolescents can. Not all adolescents and adults develop fully formal operations, but according to Piaget, all normal people have the potential to do so (Gallagher and Reid 1981).

Affective development is not independent of cognitive development, though it has been presented separately. As cognitive development reaches an upper limit with full attainment of formal operations, so too does affective development. The major affective constructions during the stage of formal operations build upon those of the concrete operational stage. The development of *normative feelings*, *autonomy*, and *will* during concrete operations leads to the construction of *idealistic feelings* and the development of *personality* during formal operations. Personality formation has its roots in the child's organization of autonomously constructed rules and values. Personality reflects the individual's efforts to adapt to the social world of adulthood. It is, in part, a submission of the "self" to discipline.

Moral reasoning similarly reaches full development with the attainment of formal operations. Rules are understood as necessary for cooperation. Lying is viewed as wrong because it breaks trust. Justice comes to be understood in relation to intentions. Proper punishments for social transgressions are viewed as those based on equity.

Piaget suggested that the normal and necessary intellectual and affective developments during adolescence are useful in understanding many aspects of adolescent behavior heretofore often attributed to puberty and sexual awakening. Adolescent *egocentrism* is characterized by applying a criterion of what is logical to human and societal actions with insufficient understanding that the world is not always ordered logically and its citizens are not always logical. The adolescent, necessarily an idealist of sorts, explores, in thought and conversation, ways to reform society. These developments, in Piaget's view, are brought on, not by puberty, but by the normal and necessary intellectual and affective developments that take place during the acquisition of formal operations.

A final *equilibrium* is attained only when the adolescent strives to enter the adult world and works at a "real" job. This effort necessarily generates disequilibrium as the logical adolescent is confronted with the views of others who have adapted their reasoning to a world not always ordered so simply.

NOTES

1. In Chapter 5 it was mentioned that concrete operational children use the two reversibilities—inversion and reciprocity—in solving conservation problems. They can mentally reverse by inversion or reciprocity (compensation), though they cannot coordinate the use of inversion and reciprocity. in formal operational thought, children learn to coordinate the two reversibilities. In the balance problem (page 151), inversion and reciprocity are seen when a child understands that equal weights at equal distance from the fulcrum effectively cancel each other, or establish balance. In addition, children use reciprocity when they recognize that a small weight placed farther from the fulcrum compensates for a larger weight placed closer. Thus, where the two reversibility operations were previously used independently, in formal thought they function together in a coordinated manner.

2. For our purposes in this section, adolescence is thought of as roughly from age 15 to age 18, and the adolescent is assumed to have developed formal operations.

Chapter 7

THE IMPLICATIONS OF INTELLECTUAL AND AFFECTIVE DEVELOPMENT

Earlier chapters have presented an introduction to Piaget's theory of cognitive and affective development as it relates to the development of the child. The basic elements of Piaget's work have been discussed, though they have not been examined in detail. A realistic and complete evaluation of Piaget's theory cannot be made solely on the material in this book.

An attempt has been made to trace the development of the structures of intelligence from birth through adulthood and to establish the relation between early sensorimotor development and later development. Piaget's theory clearly has suggested that the path of cognitive development is the same for all people. A descriptive outline of cognitive development has emerged.

SUMMARY OF THE STAGES OF DEVELOPMENT

During the sensori-motor stage (0–2 years), an infant's reflexive behaviors gradually evolve into clearly intelligent behavior. Through maturation and active interaction with

172

the environment (assimilation and accommodation), sensori-motor behaviors become increasingly differentiated and progressively evolve into intentional behaviors. The infant develops means-end problem-solving behavior. By age 2, a child is able mentally to represent objects and events, and mentally (through representation) to arrive at solutions to sensori-motor problems. The schemata of a two-year-old are qualitatively and quantitatively superior to those of a younger child. By age 2, affective development can be seen in children's likes and dislikes. Affect is largely invested in the self.

During the preoperational stage (2–7 years), intellectual behavior moves from the sensori-motor level to the conceptual level. There is a rapid development of representational skills including spoken language, which accompanies the rapid conceptual development of the period. The development of spoken language is *not* necessary for the development of reasoning to proceed. A child's thought is egocentric in that, unable to assume the viewpoints of others, he (or she) believes that everything he thinks is correct. In conservation problems he is unaware of transformations of states and tends to "center" on perceptual aspects of problems. By age 7, thought is prelogical. Conflicts between perception and reasoning are generally resolved in favor of perception. Representation and language development facilitate the beginnings of true social behavior. Moral feelings and moral reasoning make their appearance. Children begin to reason about rules and justice, but they have not yet developed a concept of intentionality.

The concrete operational child (7–11 years) develops the use of logical thought. Children can solve conservation problems and most "concrete" problems. The two reversibilities, inversion and reciprocity, are used independently in reasoning. During these years, the logical operations of seriation and classification typically develop. The child can think logically, but cannot apply logic to hypothetical and abstract problems. The major affective developments during the concrete operational stage are the development of the *will* and the beginning of *autonomous* thought. These

Table 7.1
Summary of the Stages of Cognitive Development

Stage	Characteristics of the Stage	Major Change of the Stage
Sensori-motor (0–2 years)		Development proceeds from reflex activity to representation and sensori-motor solutions to problems. Primitive likes and dislikes emerge. Affect invested in the "self"
Period 1 (0–1 months)	Reflex activity only; no differentiation	
Period 2 (1–4 months)	Hand-mouth coordination; differentiation via sucking reflex	
Period 3 (4–8 months)	Hand-eye coordination; repeats unusual events	
Period 4 (8–12 months)	Coordination of two schemata; object permanence attained	
Period 5 (12–18 months)	New means through experimentation—follows sequential displacements	
Period 6	Internal representation; new means through	

Stage		
Preoperational (2–7 years)	Problems solved through representation—language development (2–4 years). Thought and language both egocentric. Cannot solve conservation problems	Development proceeds from sensori-motor representation to prelogical thought and solutions to problems. True social behavior begins. Intentionality absent in moral reasoning
Concrete operations (7–11 years)	Reversability attained. Can solve conservation problems—logical operations developed and applied to concrete problems. Cannot solve complex verbal problems and hypothetical problems	Development proceeds from prelogical thought to logical solutions to concrete problems. Development of the will and beginnings of autonomy appear. Intentionality is constructed
Formal operations (11–15 years)	Logically solves all types of problems—thinks scientifically. Solves complex verbal and hypothetical problems. Cognitive structures mature	Development proceeds from logical solving of concrete problems to logical solving of all classes of problems. Emergence of idealistic feelings and personality formation. Adaptation to adult world begins

developments are instrumental in the increased regulation and stability of affective thought, which begins at this time. In addition, the construction of a concept of intentionality emerges and allows children to begin to consider the motives of others when making moral judgments.

During the stage of formal operations (11–15 years), cognitive structures (schemata) become qualitatively "mature." A child becomes structurally able to apply logical operations to all classes of problems. The child can apply logical thought to hypothetical problems and problems involving the future. The child with formal operations can operate on the logic of an argument independent of its content. Logic becomes firmly available to the child as a tool of thought. During adolescence, formal thought is characterized by egocentrism. An adolescent tries to reduce all reasoning behavior to what is logical and has difficulty coordinating his or her ideals with what is real. Idealistic feelings emerge. Personality formation begins as the adolescent begins to adapt the "self" to the adult world.

At each new level of cognitive development, previous levels are incorporated and integrated. A preoperational child does not discard earlier sensori-motor schemata and take up new ones. Sensori-motor schemata are modified and improved. The processes of assimilation and accommodation permit the continuous *construction* of cognitive structures. Schemata are continually modified throughout life, from birth onward. While changes in capabilities for logical reasoning cease after the development of formal operations, changes in content and function of intelligence continue. That is, people continue to develop concepts, areas of content, and purposes to which their reasoning can be applied.

Thus, early sensori-motor development is the foundation on which later conceptual development is built. The basic paradigm of cognitive development for Piaget is the assimilation and accommodation of experience, resulting in qualitative structual changes in cognitive structures (schemata). All knowledge is constructed by the child. In this sense, the child is truly father to the man.

CHARACTERISTICS OF COGNITIVE DEVELOPMENT STAGES

In this book Piaget's theory is outlined as four major stages across the *continuum* of development. Each stage is further divided into smaller substages. Every major change in development is one more step on the way to formal reasoning. Each step represents a qualitative change in reasoning abilities. Advances always share certain characteristics:

1. Each advance is characterized by qualitatively different reasoning. The reasoning of successive stages or periods within a stage is always superior to the reasoning of previous stages or periods.
2. Each stage or improvement in reasoning permeates a child's reasoning rather than affects reasoning about a particular event. For example, the child who constructs a concept that the length of objects does not change when the position of the object changes (conservation of length) can use this new reasoning in situations where object length is relevant. Objects and space literally take on a new dimension for the child. Many structures are affected, not just one isolated structure.
3. Each new advance involves an integration and extension of the knowledge and reasoning of the previous level into "new" knowledge. Structures, or schemata, are changed (through adaptation), but prior formulations are never destroyed or eliminated. What was previously known remains with some improvement in the quality of knowledge. Each new level of reasoning is a *transformation* of prior reasoning and as such is not totally *new*; rather, it is *improved*.
4. The stages of development are invariant. Formal reasoning cannot develop before concrete opera-

tions are developed. Concrete operations develop only after preoperational reasoning develops. Development always progresses from a less differentiated and less sophisticated level of reasoning to a more differentiated and more sophisticated level of reasoning.

5. Each advance in reasoning is accompanied by egocentrism in the initial use of new reasoning. Preoperational children initially view their thoughts as necessarily correct. This egocentrism of thought diminishes gradually as children recognize that peers and others have ideas that conflict with their own. This raises doubts about the certainty of their own ideas. Those with formal opertions are initially egocentric in that they judge the correctness of thoughts against a criterion of logic of reasoning. This egocentrism gradually diminishes when (and if) the individuals implement their views in a real way—typically, by getting a job.

INTELLIGENCE AND ADAPTATION

For Piaget, cognitive development is the intellectual counterpart of biological adaptation to the environment. As we adapt biologically to our environment, so too do we adapt intellectually. Through assimilation and accommodation, the external world is organized and given structure. Schemata are the products of the organization and construction.

Adaptation begins at birth with the exercise of sensorimotor reflexes. Differentiations via reflexes (sucking, grasping) are some of the first adaptations. As a child develops, the adaptations he or she makes becomes less related to sensory and motor behaviors and, to the untrained eye, are less clearly seen as adaptations.

The concept of adaptation is a concept of motivation. Adaptations occur when there is a "need" or a value to the individual. The major source of the "need" for adaptation is *disequilibrium*. Adaptations, including intellectual adaptations, are neither automatic nor inevitable. The minds of children do not develop until they see some intellectual value *to them*; that is, until *they* experience disequilibrium.

VARIABLES IN COGNITIVE DEVELOPMENT

The critical variables in cognitive development are maturation, experience, social interaction, and equilibration. Piaget used these terms in a general, not a specific, way. He avoided the fruitless nature-nurture argument whether intelligence is inherited (maturation) or learned (experience) by maintaining that each of the above variables is necessary for cognitive development but that *none alone is sufficient* to assure its occurrence. According to Piaget, the *interaction* of all four sets the course of development.

Two of the variables, maturation and equilibration,[1] are usually not subject to any external control. The other two variables, experience and social interaction, are in part determined by external events. Experiential and social situations can be structured so that the child has opportunities to act on things and interact with others. Piaget recognized the potential disequilibrating effect of the "right" experience at the "right" time. While such structuring can be done, whether these experiences are assimilated and accommodated is not ensured by the structuring because these processes are controlled by equilibration, an internal process. The saying "You can lead a horse to water, but you can't make him drink" is appropriate here.

The question whether schooling (a form of experience) can affect structural development is an important one. Few would argue that schooling does not affect cognitive *content* and *function*. Children acquire information (content) in school that they might not encounter otherwise (for example, the study of history, science, and English grammar). Also, children generally develop skills in applying knowledge (function), such as acquiring computational skills in arithmetic. These may be acquired *with or without* comprehension, depending on the availability of the relevant structures necessary for comprehension at the time of "learning" the instruction. Regarding structure, most studies conclude that children attain concrete operations around age 6 or 7 regardless of formal schooling. A number of studies report that the development of formal operations is much more related to schooling than are earlier levels of development.

Thus it would seem that schooling, *as it is traditionally carried out*, plays a more important role in helping children acquire content and functions to which they can apply reasoning and knowledge (structures) than it does in aiding the development of structures. Also, the importance of schooling and experience in general in developing cognitive structures *may be* more important in later than earlier periods.

KNOWLEDGE AND REALITY: A CONSTRUCTION

The developing child's knowledge of the world (and reality) is not a copy of the "objective" world. Each individual, over the course of his or her development, constructs knowledge and reality (through assimilation and accommodation). Physical, logical-mathematical, and social-arbitrary knowledge are not acquired directly but are *constructed* by the individual child.

> The clearest result of our research on the psychology of intelligence is that even the structures most necessary to the adult mind, such as the logico-mathematical structures, are not innate in the child; they are built up little by little. . . . There are no innate structures: every structure presupposes a construction. All these constuctions originate from prior structures and revert, in the final analysis . . . to the biological problem. (Piaget 1967, pp. 149–50)

Some may question whether knowledge is a construction; most children around the same age, and most adults, seem to have similar concepts. Although it is true that many people have similar concepts, this does not make the notion of construction less viable. The world we live in is a physical and social world containing a diversity of objects. For most children, wherever they live, the necessary physical ingredients are present to enable them to construct physical and logical-mathematical knowledge. For example, most children encounter trees and other plants. They have active experiences with trees, and so structures of trees are constructed. Because there are certain physical similarities and differences among trees, children "discover" and construct similar schemata of trees. It is therefore reasonable to expect children who live in the same or a similar environment to construct similar physical knowledge. Children reared in different environments, where the raw materials for the construction of similar concepts are not present, cannot be expected to develop similar structures. For example, Eskimo children may never see a tree growing. If their only source of wood is driftwood found in the ocean, this may become the material from which concepts of trees are built. Thus an Eskimo child or adult may have a concept of wood and tree as being rootless, leafless, and so on. Virtually any environment contains potential experiences and materials that permit the construction of logical-mathematical structures such as number, length, and volume. Number requires that children act on sets of objects. The objects can be checkers, stones, sticks, whatever. The particular materials are not important; what is important is that collections be available for manipulation.

The development of cognitive structures and knowledge is an evolutionary process that takes place within every individual; it is manifest in the individual's schemata, which are constantly undergoing change. The process of assimilation ensures that schemata will not be copies of reality; accommodation ensures that constructions will have a measure of correspondence to the real world (Elkind 1969, p. 329).

NOTES

1. Maturation is generally viewed as not affected by experience. In reality, such things as diet and nutrition can affect maturation. While equilibration is under internal control, experiences are frequently necessary to permit equilibration to take place.

Chapter 8

THE IMPLICATIONS OF PIAGET'S THEORY FOR EDUCATION

This chapter deals with some of the clear implications of Piaget's theory for educational practice and for understanding children. Piaget did not direct his research toward education and teaching, but his theory of how children acquire knowledge and develop intellectually clearly provides much that is relevant to education. Many psychologists and educators have interpreted and applied Piagetian theory over the past fifteen years, and some general implications for education are relatively clear. The application of Piagetian theory to educational practice necessitates that it be translated into applied settings. Obviously this requires considerable familiarity with the theory, much more than can be presented in a single book.

Most of us who are interested in interpreting Piaget's work for educators consider the "cookbook" approach, one that attempts to tell teachers what to do, to be inappropriate. Piaget's theory *cannot* be reduced to a set of operational procedures. Piaget's theory is *one* perspective on which to reflect that can be used to aid teachers in understanding children and why they do or do not learn in school. Educators who come to understand Piaget's work will find ways to integrate it into their dealings with children. With this in mind, the implications suggested here are general and not specific.

STAGES VERSUS CONTINUUM

It seems important to keep in mind that as much as I and others write about stages in Piaget's theory, development is viewed as a continuous process. Stages are useful for conceptualizing development and thinking about the characteristics of reasoning of children at various points along the continuum of development. Stages can be a trap for our thinking. Ten years ago, Piagetians and practitioners focused on movement from stage to stage. The broader and more important issue is, "How do we encourage development?"

DEVELOPMENT AND LEARNING

The word "development" has been used extensively throughout this book, and the word "learning" has occurred rarely. Development and learning have similarities and differences.

Intellectual, or cognitive, *development* is the process of growth of intellectual structures. It is viewed as a process of construction. The interaction of maturation, experience, social interaction, and equilibration are all important.

Two usages or meanings of the word "learning" are differentiated by Piagetians. The first usage can be called learning in the broad sense, and it is synonymous with development. It is appropriate to talk about the *development of*, or the *learning of*, physical knowledge, logical-mathematical knowledge, and social arbitrary knowledge. The second usage of learning is narrower. It refers to the acquisition of *specific information* from the environment, learning that is assimilated into an existing schema. Most content learning is of this second kind. Both forms of learning imply comprehension (Wadsworth 1978; Gallagher and Reid 1981).

Rote memory, or memorization, is not considered learning because it does not involve assimilation and comprehension. Some theories, such as behaviorism, consider rote memory as a form of learning and do not differentiate between it and the two kinds of learning defined here. For Piagetians, learning always involves construction and comprehension.[1]

Invariance of Concept Acquisition: When to Teach

Piaget stated that cognitive structures (schemata) are developed in an invariant sequence.[2] That is, the course of cognitive development, marked by the development of structures, is the same for all children, although the ages at which they attain particular structures may vary with intelligence and the social environment (Piaget and Inhelder 1969, p. 153). Invariance is most clearly described in this book in the discussions of sensori-motor intelligence (Chapter 3) and the attainment of conservation skills (Chapters 4 and 5). Research on the invariance concept, while not conclusive, supports Piaget's belief that acquisition of concepts is hierarchical and integrative in nature (Dasen 1977).

A word of caution: Piaget did not say that the sequence of cognitive development he described is the only sequence in which schemata can be acquired. In fact, he indicated that other sequences are possible (Bringuier 1980, p. 100; and see Question 3, Chapter 9). Piaget described cognitive development; he did not determine how it *must* proceed. He did not preclude other sequences, though any other sequence would have to meet the criterion that successive structures incorporate previous structures in an integrative and hierarchical fashion.

Assuming that concept acquisition is invariant, at least in Western cultures, then it makes educational sense to use Piaget's model of invariance in determining *when* to expect children to know *what*. Curriculum sequences should be designed with children's changing cognitive status in mind. If curriculums do not take into account children's levels of conceptual development, learning without comprehension is going to be inefficient. Children cannot learn if they do not have the prerequisite cognitive skills.

Readiness to learn is of particular concern to educators of elementary school children, though it *should be* of concern at *all* levels of education. According to Piagetian theory, a child is cognitively "ready" to develop a particular concept when, and only when, he or she has acquired the schemata that are necessary (prerequisites). Of course, there needs to be a reason to learn (motivation).

How Knowledge Is Acquired

American educational practice is generally based on the premise that knowledge is something that can be directly transmitted from teachers and books to students. When knowledge is not acquired, there is assumed to be a problem with the student.

Possibly the most important and most revolutionary implication of Piaget's theory is that children construct knowledge from their actions on the environment. Physical knowledge is constructed through actions on objects. Legitimate concepts of trees can only be acquired from, and elaborated upon, by children's "acting on" trees. Pictures of trees, stories about trees, and reading about trees cannot develop a complete knowledge of trees in young children. Logical-mathematical knowledge is constructed from actions on objects when the most important component is the child's *action*, not the particular object. Number, length, and area concepts cannot be built up from hearing about them or reading about them. The construction of social-arbitrary knowledge is dependent on the child's action on, and interaction with, other people. Again, this form of knowledge cannot be directly transmitted through words or other symbols; it must be constructed.

For educators, the basic implication is clear. If an objective of education is to enhance children's acquisition of knowledge, educational methods need to be consistent with how children acquire knowledge. Many children do not "learn" because they literally cannot understand what they are being asked to learn.

Individual Differences

Piaget concerned himself primarily with the general psychological processes in cognitive development. He did not directly concern himself with the topic of individual differences, though the fact that differences between individuals exist is implicit in all his work. The major factor in cognitive development is the interaction of maturation, experience, social interactions, and equilibration. Clearly, different individuals can be expected to differ with respect to each of these variables. *Rate* of cognitive development can vary considerably among children.

Since development can be traced back to biological factors before birth, there can clearly be inherited biological differences that affect cognitive development. These can be manifest in different rates of *maturation* of relevant physiological structures.

Experience is a second variable in development. No two children have the same experiences. The history of experiences is different for every human being. Even identical twins, raised in the same home, cannot be assumed to have had the "same" experiences. Accordingly, differences in prior experiences can contribute to "individual differences" in cognitive development.

As children have different histories of general experiences, so do they have different histories of social experiences, or *social interaction*. Because social interaction does not become an effective variable in cognitive development until after the egocentrism of the preoperational period comes to rest, the value of interactions prior to that time is as experience, not as social interaction. After age 6 or 7, interactions assume their "social" value. Clearly one's history of interactions, whether they are as experience or social, vary, which contributes to individual differences.

Equilibration is the regulator of the relation between assimilation and accommodation. It can be thought of as a mode, or style, of regulation. A given event may be assimilated or accommodated differently by different persons. Many factors can contribute to this source of individual differences.

Children can be expected to differ in their histories of maturation, experience, social interaction, and equilibration; and they can differ in how these factors interact to govern cognitive development. A clear expectation is that wide individual differences in conceptual development can be expected even in children of the same age. Among 100 randomly selected seven- and eight-year-olds (probably second-graders), we will find that most are close to transition from preoperational reasoning to concrete operational reasoning. A smaller group will probably still be early preoperational, and another similar group will be late concrete operational. We will also find some students who are sensori-motor in their reasoning, and a few who are developing formal operations. Thus, among children close in chronological age, we can expect to find levels of development ranging from sensori-motor through early formal operational. The same range of developmental levels can be found at any chronological age. Individual differences are large. Children are certainly different in terms of the thinking, reasoning, and comprehension they bring to academic work and what they can be expected to learn and comprehend.

METHODS OF ASSESSING CONCEPTUAL DEVELOPMENT

Methods and procedures for assessing children's levels of conceptual development according to Piagetian concepts are needed. Piagetian tasks can be used for diagnostic purposes to make such an assessment. A relatively complete description of how to use Piagetian principles to assess a child's developmental level or level of knowledge development regarding a particular concept can be found in Wadsworth 1978. That book also contains complete descriptions of, and procedures for, administering twenty-nine tasks derived from Piaget's work that are suitable for children of preschool through high school age.

Conventional intelligence tests, such as the Stanford-Binet and the Wechsler scales, have been constructed by selecting items that reliably discriminate between chronological age groups. While these instruments are useful, the use of Piagetian derived scales will add an important dimension to assessing logical reasoning and thinking, something most tests do not do adequately.

The individual assessment of children by using a Piagetian scale may not always be practical or desirable. The ultimate goal, from a Piagetian perspective, is to have teachers become very familiar with Piaget's theory.[3] Once you become familiar with the theory, it becomes a frame of reference through which you can interpret children's behavior. In most cases, regular observations of children, thought about in a Piagetian framework, will in effect allow you to informally assess children's development continuously.

MOTIVATION

Children are *motivated* to restructure their knowledge when they encounter experiences that conflict with their predictions. Piaget called such an occurrence *disequilibration*, and the result of it, *disequilibrium*. Some have called it cognitive conflict. To the extent that educators are interested in helping children acquire knowledge (as it is defined here), they must develop methods that encourage disequilibrium and permit children to carry out, in their own ways, the reestablishment of equilibrium through active methods (assimilation and accommodation). How can disequilibrium be recognized and encouraged by the teacher?

Cognitive Conflict

Critical exploration is a method of questioning students that can be used by teachers (or parents) to help lead students into productive *cognitive conflict* (disequilibrium).

Such a method is adapted to educational purposes by questioning children about how they would approach a problem and how they arrived at their answers. The teacher presents children with further problems, based on those the children have already solved (or not solved), to see what rules or generalizations the children have formed. Often the children are given a second problem, especially in mathematics, that, if solved by the procedure used to solve the first problem, would lead to an incorrect answer. Thus, by setting up a conflict situation, the teacher notes whether the disturbance causes an adjustment and consequent avoidance of future errors. (Gallagher and Reid 1981, p. 150)

The purpose of critical explorations is to determine what constructions (rules and generalizations) a student has regarding the content under discussion. The teacher can then pose questions designed to conflict with the reasoning underlying the child's constructions.

For example, if a young girl is experimenting with sinking and floating objects, a teacher might ask the child which objects float and which objects sink, and why. Many children believe that objects such as wood float and metals sink. One might ask such a child, "What will happen if we put a needle on the water?" or "What will happen if we put a metal box in the water?" Children who believe that metals sink under all conditions will probably predict that the needle and box will sink. Trying out these beliefs, the child will find that they float. Experiences such as these, guided by teachers' questions, necessarily produce cognitive conflict.

Social Interactions

Peer interactions become important for cognitive development when a child becomes able to assimilate the viewpoints of others when they are found to be different from his or her own. This comes about when the egocentrism of preoperational thought is dispelled, around age 6 or 7. Accordingly, peer interactions are of cognitive importance from the time the child enters school. Children learn to evaluate their egocentric thoughts by comparing them to the thoughts of others. Around the age of 6 or 7, most children become able to accommodate to the views of others. Thus peer interactions can be a fruitful means of stimulating natural *cognitive conflicts* that can generate accommodation to the views of others and an evaluation of one's own concepts. Social-arbitrary knowledge, a form of knowledge created by humans, is constructed by children from their social interactions. Social-arbitrary knowledge cannot be acquired independent of other people (physical and logical-mathematical knowledge can). To the extent that educational programs purport to "teach" social knowledge, legitimate opportunities for social interaction must be provided.

One peer activity of great value that is frequently overlooked by teachers is children tutoring (or teaching) other children. Gallagher and Reid (1981) point out that benefits acrue to both the tutor and the tutee when students attempt to communicate their points of view. Tutors learn to clarify their thinking and tutees experience cognitive conflict from being exposed to the views of peer tutors.

Any situation in school that involves peer interaction is legitimate: role playing, games, play, and so one. They all stimulate peer interaction. Interactions can be centered on pertinent concepts. Conceptual development can be facilitated by making use of peer activities.

Spontaneous Interests and Surprise

In an earlier book I suggested that children be permitted to explore many of their *spontaneous interests* (Wadsworth 1978). Such interests, unique to the individual child, frequently reflect disequilibrium and are sources of motivation. When children communicate a strong interest in something, they are frequently communicating to us as parents or teachers that the area of interest has generated cognitive conflict for them. We all know that when we can concentrate on things *we are really* interested in, our efforts are more intense and more productive than when we work on things that are of lesser interest. It is of value in education to legitimize the role of spontaneous interests, and interests in general, in the school day. Spontaneous interests can be viewed legitimately as part of the child's "lesson plans" of development. Teachers can find ways to permit children to investigate their spontaneous interests for some portion of their school time. It is reasonable for educators to view time spent on spontaneous interests as valid for intellectual development and knowledge acquisition.

Another approach I suggested earlier is for teachers to use *surprise* to induce disequilibrium (ibid.). Teachers cannot predict what will function as a "surprise" for all students, but they can structure experiences to have outcomes that teachers expect are not predictable by most students. The unknown and the unpredictable can generate both interest and cognitive conflict.

When I was in elementary school, the teacher of our combined 5–8 class put our whole K-8 school (45 children) on a bus, and we drove off to see a whale grounded on a beach a few miles away (on Long Island). None of us had ever seen a real whale before, and we were indeed "surprised" by this novel experience.

> We looked at it, we listened to it, we went up to it to touch it (it could not move much), we ran away from it when it opened its massive mouth, we threw water on it, we made faces at it—we did all sorts of things. From that day on we all knew exactly what a whale was. (Ibid., pp. 54–55)

FOSTERING MORAL REASONING

Can parents do anything to help foster, or at least not to interfere with, the development of moral judgment? Piaget has showed us how and under what conditions moral concepts are *constructed*. If the goals of education (at home and in school) include the development of sound moral reasoning, cooperation, and autonomy, and if we agree with Piaget's views, we can conclude that the authoritarian model for the relationship between children and adults is a poor one.[4] If children develop moral judgment, cooperation, and self-discipline in an authoritarian environment, it is *in spite of*, not as a result of, their authoritarian relationship with adults.

> It is ... absurd and even immoral to wish to impose upon the child a fully worked-out system of discipline when the social life of children themselves is sufficiently developed to give rise to a discipline infinitely nearer to the inner submission which is the mark of adult morality. It is idle ... to try and transform the child's mind from outside, when his own taste for active research and his desire for cooperation suffice to ensure a normal intellectual development. The adult must therefore be a collaborator and not a master, from this double point of view, moral and rational. (Piaget 1965, p. 404)

Piaget recommended that schools foster active interactions between children, much in the way John Dewey (1963) described in the early 1900s. Authoritarian teachers need to discover ways to modify their authoritarian role so that a major portion of their interaction with children can be as collaborators and "equals." The development of cooperation by a child, as well as the development of self-discipline (autonomy) can occur only in an environment that permits it.

As with other knowledge, children *construct* moral knowledge and reasoning out of their *actions* in the environment. The leap from psychological theory to educational practice is a large one. Piaget recognized this.

> ... it is one thing to prove that cooperation in the play and spontaneous social life in children brings about certain moral effects, and another to establish the fact that this cooperation can be universally applied as a method of education. (Ibid., p. 406)

Neither Piaget nor any other psychologist or educator can provide the teacher or parent with a ready-made plan that will ensure children's development of moral reasoning. Common sense suggests that educational practice at home and in school should be consistent with what we know about children and their development. What follows are several guidelines consistent with Piaget's theory:

1. Teachers and parents can assume nonauthoritarian relationships with children for at least some of their time together. Teachers can encourage children to resolve issues themselves and develop autonomy.

2. When punishment of children is necessary, it can be based on reciprocity rather than expiation. For example, the boy who refuses to clean up his room can be deprived of the things he does not clean up. The girl who hits other children can be denied interaction with other children.

3. Teachers can foster social interaction in their classrooms and encourage questioning and examining any issue children may raise. There is *intellectual* value in dealing with children's *spontaneous* intellectual interests, and it is equally valuable to their moral development to deal with spontaneous moral questions.

4. Teachers can engage students, even at the preschool level, in discussions of moral issues. As children listen to their peers' views, they can experience cognitive *disequilibration*, which can lead to a reorganization of their concepts. Cognitive conflict is necessary for the restructuring of reasoning (development) to proceed.

5. Schools and classrooms can be restructured to allow students greater participation in the *valid* aspects of the school-governing process. Although many "educators" would like to think otherwise, responsibility, cooperation, and self-discipline cannot be transmitted to children authoritatively. Such concepts must be constructed by children out of their own experiences. Teachers and parents are generally the ones who structure the social environment to which children adapt and from which they learn. It is questionable whether children can develop

concepts of justice based on cooperation in an environment established on justice based only on authority.

TEACHING METHODS AND MATERIALS: HOW TO TEACH

Piaget's theory suggested that teaching methods and materials should be consistent with children's levels of conceptual development. *Active physical and mental interactions* of the child with the environment (physical and social interactions) that permit *construction* are seen as the most important school-related factor in cognitive development. The act of constructing is the essence of intellectual development. Regarding school experiences and cognitive development, Piaget wrote:

> Experience is always necessary for intellectual development ... but I fear that we may fall into the illusion that being submitted to an experience (a demonstration) is sufficient for a subject to disengage the structure involved. But more than this is required. The subject must be active, must transform things, and find the structure of his own actions on the objects. (Piaget 1964, p. 4)

Cognitive reorganization resulting from assimilation and accommodation can come about only through the actions of the child. Thus actions, physical or cognitive, must occur if cognitive reorganization is going to take place. It must also be remembered that, according to Piaget, assimilation and accommodation of actions are always under internal control (equilibration), and the reorganization of cognitive structures in a particular way can never be ensured by external organization of experience.

Throughout the stage of concrete operations, the manipulation of objects and materials dealing with concepts to be learned is most important. Seriation schemata ($A < B$, $B < C$, thus $A < C$) can best be developed with concrete operational objects employing the concepts to be learned. In a similar manner, equivalence concepts ($A = B$, $B = C$, thus $A = C$) can best be learned if the child acts on objects that employ the concept. Reversibility in mathematical operations can be facilitated in children's learning if problems in multiplication and division are placed in opposition to one another (initially using concrete materials such as blocks) (14×3 _____; $42 - 3$ _____; $42 - 14$ _____). The same principle holds true for reversibility learnings in simple addition and subtraction. Problems placed in opposition demonstrate reversibility and help facilitate accommodation to the concept ($5 + 4$ _____; $9 - 4$ _____; $9 - 5$ _____). Throughout the concrete operational stage, concrete experiences that result in reflective abstraction generate conceptual development.

With the attainment of formal operations, children become able to develop some logical-mathematical concepts without the aid of direct physical experience. At this level, the activity of the child can be purely representational and independent of any "concrete" experience. The child can act on or reflect on verbally presented conceptual material. Conceptual development can proceed based on the child's actions on written and verbal materials. Of course, even the adolescent or adult with formal operations continues to use concrete experience in the development of concepts and continues to need concrete experiences in order to develop *new* physical knowledge. If one has never had any experience with sailboats, it is difficult to acquire any useful knowledge about them.

EDUCATIONAL INTERVENTION AND PIAGET

There is great concern in educational circles as to whether educational intervention offers a solution to the problems of the "disadvantaged" and other deprived groups of children. Can conceptual development be speeded up? Can early intervention (preschool) compensate for social-class differences in academic "readiness"? Piaget's theory of cognitive development does not provide a clear answer to these questions. Development is a function of the inter-action of maturation, experience, social interaction, and equilibration. Presumably, within the limitations of mat-uration and equilibration, experiences (both social and gen-eral) can be manipulated. This does not ensure that the child will act on the elements in a situation and will assim-ilate and accommodate according to a formula. Piaget did not say how or under what specific conditions conceptual development can be advanced. In addition, the conse-quences of "artificially" advancing development are not clear. Unfortunately for education, Piaget was concerned with how concepts develop, not how to develop concepts. Fifteen years ago, authorities on Piaget's work generally suggested that early intervention and efforts to help chil-dren acquire knowledge would not be fruitful.

Today this negative conclusion has been substantially eroded. Most Piagetians believe that school experiences can have an impact on children's acquisition of knowledge *if* teaching practices are brought in line with children's ways of learning (Wadsworth 1978). Kagan (1976) provides evi-dence that some functional retardation is even reversible. Most Piagetians agree that teachers can help facilitate cog-nitive development, but most argue for an "enrichment" approach (rather than an acceleration approach) that per-mits children to solidify and generalize the knowledge they have. The long-term effects of acceleration are still not clear.

A FINAL WORD

As an educational psychologist, I feel that one of the most important determinants of teachers' behavior with respect to students is how they (the teachers) conceptualize phenomena. The classic example can be seen in the nature-nurture controversy that has pervaded psychology for years. If a teacher conceptualizes intelligence (the ability to suc-ceed in school) as "fixed," she or he is probably not going to be motivated to try very hard to help a student who is a poor performer in the classroom. On the other hand, a teacher who conceptualizes intelligence as "developed," not fixed, may be motivated to help the poor performer. How teachers conceptualize intelligence and learning will influence their actions. Teachers' expectations of how children can perform in the classroom are derived from their conceptualizations. The fact that teacher expectations (as well as parental expectations and self-expectation) are communicated to students and affect their achievement has been well documented (Rosenthal and Jacobsen 1968). How teachers conceptualize has a lot to do with how much is learned, and who learns, in their classrooms.

Piaget's conceptualizations (theory) are at once comprehensive and useful. They offer an alternative way of conceptualizing behavior and development for those interested in psychology and education. At best, psychology as a science operates on the level of theories. There are no laws in psychology (as in physics or chemistry), so one must be content with using theories and trying to find those that are most useful. All theories in psychology are constantly changing; they are being validated, tested, and reorganized. To ask if a theory is "right" or "wrong" is a poor question. Some theories are useful for explaining one phenomenon and useless for explaining another. Thus the user of theories (and conceptualizations) must pick and choose with care. Generally, the acceptance or rejection of a theory is a function of its utility in predicting behavior, its persuasive power, its logic, and its novelty. All these criteria continue to reflect the appeal of Piaget's work.

There is little doubt that Piaget's theory of cognitive development will continue to change and will become more refined, as it has over the years. Some Piagetian concepts may not stand up in the face of future research. Others certainly will. This chapter has presented an introduction to the part of Piaget's conceptualizations that seem to be most important for education. Needless to say, the implications of Piaget's concepts for education have not been exhausted by this work. My interpretations of Piaget's writings have produced some implications that are very general in nature; they are not remedies for educational problems. They are a start. Piaget's work has generated a degree of

Sensori-motor   Preoperational   Concrete   Formal

interest and inquiry that is unprecedented, and it shall continue to do so for many years.

NOTES

1. The assertion that rote memory is *not* a kind of learning does not mean that rote memory is not valued, but that it is not a part of intellectual development from a Piagetian perspective. Rote memory is a valuable and useful skill to be encouraged for its own sake. But memorization and comprehension are not the same thing. The child who comprehends mathematical operations is intellectually different from the child who has only memorized computational procedures.

2. Piaget never made any claim that his theory applied universally (Dasen 1977). The universality of his theory is speculation on the part of others.

3. One of the best ways to understand Piaget's theory more fully is to practice administering Piagetian tasks to children under the supervision of someone experienced in this method (usually in a college course).

4. This is not an argument against adults exerting their authority over children when it is appropriate, but children cannot be expected to develop advanced moral reasoning while authority remains the dominant moral force in their lives.

Chapter 9

QUESTIONS
AND
ANSWERS

Question 1: Is the sensori-motor stage the most important stage in intellectual development? If children do not make normal progress at this stage, does it have an effect on intellectual potential?

Answer: The answer to both questions is no. Piagetian theory does not contain any "critical periods," as many other theories do. Benjamin Bloom (1964) has argued that the largest percent of a child's intelligence is developed by age 8, suggesting that the early years are "critical." From a different perspective, psychoanalytic theory views the first few years of life as instrumental in determining later development. For Piaget, there is no stage or place on the continuum of development that is more important than any other.

Rates of development can speed up or slow down. There is evidence that many children who develop slowly during their early years can "catch up" by age 12 or so (Kagen 1975; Wadsworth 1978). There can be reasons why some may not catch up, but the point is that a slow rate of development during the early years (or any years) does not automatically have a detrimental or restrictive effect on later development.

Barbel Inhelder published *The Diagnosis of Reasoning in the Mentally Retarded* originally in 1943 (English translation 1968). Inhelder's book is a classic and reviews her research on the topic of retardation from the perspective of Piagetian theory. In this still current work, Inhelder points out that some children have slower than average rates of development and may be classified as retarded on other criteria, but they are capable of achieving formal operations. These individuals she labels *pseudo-retarded* (see Figure 9.1) and calls them slow learners: ". . . the slow learner is capable of achieving formal operations and thus in time of reaching the full development of a normal child" (p. 293).

Thus it is clearly the case that some children with slower than average rates of development do have the potential for developing formal operations. Below-average rates of development do not necessarily predict below-average potential.

Question 2: Is development, as Piaget describes it, universal?

Answer: Piaget did not claim that any aspect of his theory was universal. The suggestion that Piaget's theory may be universal has been made by others. Piaget found the course of development to be the same in all the children he studied, but he did not claim that it was necessarily the same in *all* children. On the other hand, there are many indicators that Piaget's theory *may* in large part be universally applicable, at least in Western cultures where it has been studied most.

The ultimate answer to the universality of Piaget's theory (or any theory) can come only after extensive cross-cultural research that examines development in many cul-

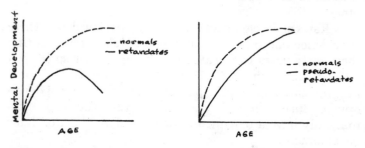

FIGURE 9.1 Developmental curves characteristic of normals, retardates, and pseudo-retardates (adapted from Inhelder 1966, p. 296).

tures and subcultures. Considerable work in this direction has been done in the last fifteen years (Dasen 1977; Berry and Dasen 1974). Dasen says that it is premature to expect an answer to the question of the universality of Piaget's theory, though Dasen does indicate that, in his judgment, at least some aspects of Piaget's theory will be found to be universal (1977, p. 10).

Question 3: Is there only one course of development, as Piaget's theory suggests?

Answer: Piaget never claimed that the course of development outlined in his theory was the only possible one (Wadsworth 1971). Yet there is considerable evidence that children do develop in the way Piaget outlined, at least in Western cultures. In an interview Piaget said:

> The problem was whether there is only one possible line of evolution in the development of knowledge or whether there may be different routes, which, of course, will lead to common points sooner or later. Well, Garcia,[1] who is quite familiar with Chinese science, thinks they have travelled a route very different from our own. So I decided to see whether it is possible to imagine a psychogenesis different from our own, which would be that of the Chinese child during the greatest period of Chinese science, and I think that it is possible. (Bringuier 1980, p. 100)

Thus Piaget argued that routes of development other than the one he outlined in his theory are possible.

Question 4: Are the relative contributions of heredity and environment constant over the course of development?

Answer: One should recognize that the exact contributions of heredity and envirnment to development are not clear. When asked about the role of heredity, Piaget said:

> It's very difficult to say, because from the time the maturation of the nervous system was first discussed, no one has ever been able to put a finger on

something really hereditary. We are sure that heredity plays a role throughout, that maturation as a factor is entirely present all the time; but nothing positive can be said about what it contributes. It offers
possibilities. We know that a certain behavior,
impossible at one degree of maturation, becomes
possible later, but we cannot say, "This is hereditary,
this is not." (Ibid., p. 39)

While it is not possible to specify exactly the contributions of heredity and environment to development, there
is agreement that they both play a role. There is also agreement that sensori-motor development is much more certain
than the development of formal operations. This argues that
the environment may play an increasing role and heredity
a decreasing role as development proceeds (Wadsworth 1978;
Flavell 1971). Piaget indicated that he believed surround-
ings become more important with age (Bringuier 1980, p.
34).

Question 5: What does Piaget have to say about memory?

Answer: The structures of the brain that memory draws on
are *schemata*. Within these structures resides that which
can be recalled or remembered or brought to conscious
awareness.

For Piaget, what is "remembered" is *not* a copy of
reality, or an exact copy of past experiences, but is derived
from the child's *construction* of the experience being
remembered.

What we've found in studying the stages of
memory in operatory problems is that the child
remembers what he's been shown as he understands
it and not as he's seen or perceived or lived it. (Ibid.,
p. 119)

For Piaget, what one remembers relevant to an event is
based on one's *current* construction of that event. If one
refers to the discussion of seriation in Chapter 5, one sees
that children's memories of events change (improve) over

time, even though the events remembered are not experienced again. Constructions improve, and memory improves without further experience with the event.

Piaget stated that there are no "pure" memories; no memories are totally accurate representations of events. To illustrate this point, he told the following story:

> . . . I have a childhood memory of my own that would be absolutely splendid if it were authentic, because it goes back to an age when one usually doesn't have memories of childhood. I was still in a baby carriage, taken out by a nurse, and she took me down the Champs-Elysees, near Rond-Point. I was the object of an attempted kidnapping. Someone tried to grab me out of the buggy. The straps held me in and the nurse scuffled with the man, who scratched her forehead; something worse might have happened if a policeman hadn't come by just then. I can see him now as if it were yesterday . . . and the man fled. That's the story. As a child I had the glorious memory of having been the object of an attempted kidnapping. Then—I must have been about fifteen—my parents received a letter from the nurse, saying that she had just been converted and wanted to confess all her sins, and that she had invented the kidnapping story herself, that she had scratched her own forehead, and that she now offered to return the watch she'd been given in recognition of her courage. In other words there wasn't an iota of truth in the memory. And I have a very vivid memory of the experience, even today. I can tell you just where it happened on the Champs-Elysees, and I can see the whole thing. . . My mother must have told someone that an attempt had been made to kidnap me . . . I overheard the story, and starting from that, I reconstituted the image—such a beautiful image that even today it seems a memory of something I experienced. . . .
>
> Now, suppose the memory had been accurate, that everything happened just as the nurse told it. It still wouldn't be a direct memory, but a reconstituted memory—reconstituted by means of the story I heard later. So I'm fairly skeptical of childhood

memories. I know that the way a child reconstitutes his childhood memories, or an adult reconstitutes his childhood memories, can be useful psychoanalytically.[2] But ultimately, I don't think there are pure memories; they always presuppose a greater or lesser degree of inference. (Ibid., pp. 120–22)

Question 6: Can people regress, or go backward, in development?

Answer: Piaget believed that when there was successful assimilation of experience, there was no regression. He also believed there could be what he called "temporary regression." When a new experience cannot be assimilated immediately, when reequilibration does not occur quickly, there may be regression in the form of a return to a more primitive level of reasoning. This is temporary until equilibration is established. Piaget offered the following example of temporary regression.

> Take the famous story of Driesch, in biology, who discovered regulation in the development of the embryo at the level of the blastula. He discovered that by cutting the egg in half he got two embryos; he was so astounded that he didn't believe it could be explained by the schemes of causal embryology, and he went back to Aristotle's ideas! He began to talk about entelechy and finally quit biology to become a philosophy professor. In my humble opinion, that's a slight regression. . . . In any case, the appeal to entelechy is a regression. Driesch's discovery was the point of departure for all causal embryology, but Driesch's theory was abandoned immediately. (Ibid., p. 47)

Question 7: Does Piaget's theory have any implications for children with learning problems and special needs?

Answer: Piaget developed his theory from work with normal children. His interest was in understanding how knowledge develops, not in individual differences. Thus, Piaget did little to contribute directly to this area. Others, working with Piagetian theory, have conducted research bearing on individual difference issues, and the theory itself has several implications.

Barbel Inhelder, a student and co-worker of Piaget, studied development of reasoning in the retarded, and her work remains a major contribution to this field (Inhelder 1968). The limited research that has been done to relate Piaget's theory to special populations is summarized in Gallagher and Reid (1981).

> What can be said with reasonable confidence is that all children with learning problems, except possibly for the seriously emotionally disturbed, follow the same course in developing intellectually as do normal children. (p. 171)

Thus, development proceeds in the same stage and substage sequence described by Piaget.

In any age group, rates of development, as well as current levels of development, vary considerably. It is expected that among a sample of 9- or 10-year-olds, most will be concrete operational, some will be entering formal operations, and some will be preoperational. Wide distributions of levels are expected at every age level. Nine- or ten-year-olds who are still preoperational or early concrete operational probably have slower than average rates of development. They may seem to be "slow learners." Certainly their capabilities for mastering content with comprehension is different from that of more advanced children at their age.

A rate of development slower than average does not necessarily mean that one is not capable of developing fully formal operations. In her study of retarded children, Inhelder suggested that some children's rates of development were slow almost from birth and that their development never advanced beyond concrete operations (1968). Such cases depict true retardation. The rate of development is slow, and formal operations are never achieved. Others start at and maintain a slower than average rate throughout development but go on to develop formal operations. These cases she called "pseudo-retardation," or slow learners. Both develop slowly, but their potentials are very different.

Bovet observes that one's rate of development can vary over life:

> Both a slowing-up and an acceleration of the developmental rate has been observed in cross-cultural and learning studies. Slowing up may be caused by lack of stimulation, and acceleration can be achieved, within certain limits, by teaching methods which closely follow the normal course of development. (Bovet 1976, p. 277)

It is probably the case that many children labeled slow learners or who have special needs in schools are the children Inhelder calls pseudo-retarded. They have slower than average rates of development but have the potential to develop formal operations. They will not usually be able to compete successfully in academic learning with average and above-average children. The educational challenge is to provide these children with rates of development that are slower than average, that is, with developmentally appropriate schooling.

Other research by Inhelder shows that some children labeled dyslexic or aphasic lack the usual synchrony of intellectual operations and symbolic imagery. There seems to be a delay in the ability to evoke and anticipate symbolic imagery, though other aspects of intellectual functioning are normal (Inhelder and Chipman 1976).

Question 8: Does Piaget's theory have any clinical applications?

Answer: It is interesting that Piaget's theory has had widespread acceptance within cognitive developmental psychology (academic psychology) in recent years and has had very little impact on clinical psychology. On the other hand, psychoanalytic theory is the predominant theory guiding clinical practice in hospitals and clinics and currently gets little attention among academic psychologists (Keegan 1982).

The purpose of clinical psychology is to help people who are experiencing disabling effects of their behavior, both their physical behavior and mental behavior. I would argue that anything that helps us understand individuals has implications for helping those who are clinically ill. Piaget's theory is one view of how people construct knowledge and develop affectively. As such, it has considerable potential for contributing to clinical theory.

Many of Piaget's concepts have clear significance clinically. For example:

> *Egocentrism*: Many behaviors of adolescents that may be viewed as antiauthority can be seen as "normal" given the egocentrism and seemingly idealistic reasoning of those with formal operations. This understanding has potential for working with adolescents.
>
> *Personality development*: Piaget provided a view of personality development that is different than other concepts of personality development. He offered the concept of *autonomy* and its significance in personality development.

Question 9: What does Piaget's theory have to say about creativity?

Answer: Creativity is a construct (concept) for which there is no accepted definition. Some view creativity as an ability that is separate from other abilities. Others view creativity as a process. Still others view creativity as a product. There is certainly little agreement on the meaning of the term.

Creativity has a mystical quality for many people. It is also generally valued and thought to be a "good" thing to have. When it is considered an ability, it is usually thought to be inherited rather than learned.

Piaget's view is that creativity is neither a separate ability nor inborn. Every act of construction of knowledge is, for Piaget, creative.

> The development of intelligence is a continuous creation. Each stage in the development process produces something radically new, totally different from what was before. (Piaget 1981, pp. 222–23)

Why some people push forward the frontiers of knowledge and others do not seems a mystery. Howard Gruber, who worked with Piaget for a time, has as his chief interest the study of creativity.[3] His research focuses on the work of Charles Darwin and the process by which Darwin arrived at his theory of evolution. Gruber shows that Darwin constructed the concept of evolution slowly, over many years of effort, while trying to sort out the meaning of variations in animal and plant life. Darwin did not come to any sudden "insight" (Gruber 1981).

One of the most creative people of our time certainly has to be Piaget. About his own work, he said:

> A few more words on the source or origin of creativity. In the course of my life, it has happened that I have come upon one or two little ideas, and when I reflect upon the origin of these, I find there are three conditions. The first condition is to work alone, to ignore everybody else, and to mistrust every influence from the outside. . . .
>
> The second condition that I think is necessary is to read a great deal in other disciplines, not in one's own discipline. For a psychologist, for instance, it is important to read in biology, epistemology, and logic, so as to develop an interdisciplinary outlook. . . .
>
> And the third aspect I think in my case has been that I have always had in my head an adversary— that is, a school of thought whose ideas one considers to be wrong. (Piaget 1981b; p. 222)

Howard Gruber, regarding Piaget and the "common man," said:

> They have a lot in common, because . . . everyone has to create his world; at bottom, you might say, they're exactly alike. That's one of the reassuring things I've learned! The genius's memory is no different from the memory of the man on the street, but it's organized differently. It's precisely the organization of the system that is different. . . . A creative man's life is much harder; he works a good deal more.

> Piaget works all the time, all the time . . . he has
> a goal. Piaget's goal is to construct the logic of the
> human mind . . . a goal he's pursued for a long time.
> A goal that guides practically everything he does.
> The average man does not have a goal of this type.
> (Bringuier 1981, pp. 79–80)

Question 10: What does Piaget's theory have to say about sex differences in development?

Answer: Piaget did not note any sex differences in development in his research and writings. Both males and females develop intellectually in the way outlined by Piaget. If there are any *major* differences between the sexes in the rate of development or in "potential," they are not apparent from Piaget's work.

Reports of reliable sex differences by researchers using Piagetian theory are few, and appropriate conclusions are generally unclear.

> Several investigations have found sex differences
> with respect to both concrete and formal operational
> competence. . . . When this finding occurs, females
> generally perform more poorly than males. This
> result is open to two interpretations: females may
> lag behind males developmentally in the acquisition
> of competence or the differences may be the product
> of activation/utilization variables which depress the
> expression of competence. (Overton and Newman
> 1982, pp. 234–35)

Lawrence Kohlberg (1969b) has developed a theory of development of moral reasoning that builds on Piaget's theory. He has also developed a scale for measuring moral reasoning. One finding of Kohlberg and other researchers is that, on Kohlberg's scale, adolescent males score higher than adolescent females. Some have interpreted this as a genuine sex difference. Others have pointed out that Kohlberg standardized his scale using only male subjects and suggest that the scale may have a sex bias built into it. Carol Gilligan (1977) has argued that females' moral reasoning develops in a somewhat different pattern than that of males and that direct comparisons with Kohlberg's scale are not valid.

More research is needed to determine whether there are significant sex differences in development. The best conclusion or working assumption at this time is that there are no general sex differences in intellectual development as described by Piaget. Of more concern should be the wide differences within *all* groups, which are well documented.

Question 11: Is the use of computers compatible with Piaget's theory?

Answer: I am not aware that Piaget ever addressed this question. It is certainly a complex and important one. I believe Piaget would remind us that machines cannot eliminate the necessity for children *constructing* knowledge. Machines cannot do the constructing for children. This should be clear from the advent of widespread use of calculators in recent years. Machines can compute, but they cannot construct knowledge.

One computer application many educators get excited about is *programmed instruction*. In programmed instruction, the content to be learned is presented through a computer onto a television screen. In its simplest form, programmed instruction is exactly like presenting the same content in a book. Programmed instruction can also employ "gamelike" procedures that vary the presentation of content. Questions can be employed, with children's answers determining what comes next (as in "branching" programs). Proponents of programmed instruction believe that well-organized content is the key to instruction. Piaget disagreed with this view because he felt it did not properly take into account the need for the child to construct knowledge in an *active* way. Nothing ensures that programmed instruction will lead to *disequilibrium* and active assimilation and accommodation. Yet, if a child is experiencing disequilibrium and is in search of information, programmed instruction, a book, or a conversation with someone knowledgeable about the child's question are all potentially helpful in the child's construction of knowledge. The point that needs to be remembered is that knowledge is constructed only when disequilibrium or cognitive conflict has been generated *in the mind of the child.*

One can view a computer as something to be known rather than a source of instruction (as in programmed instruction). Children find "user friendly" computers and computer programs interesting, and they *can* pose valid intellectual problems as they try to figure out how they work (Hofmann 1983). Seymour Papert (1980) presents an argument for the use of computers within the Piagetian tradition. Papert, who worked with Piaget, believes that when children are confronted with a computer, and when they are engaged in trying to figure out how it works, they are constructing knowledge. Papert has devised a computer program called Logo that allows children as young as three or four years of age to interact with a computer.[4]

Computer programs such as Logo seem to be universally attractive to children. They allow children to "play" with the computer, or to engage in "hacking."[5] The potential educational advantage of Logo and similar programs is that they encourage (require) children to analyze "machine" thinking in order to make the computer do the things they want done. This is an active process of construction of knowledge about machine language.

Asked about computers and children's epistemologist behaviors, Papert said:

> I had a very nice example the other day in
> school when a first grade child wanted to program
> the computer system to make objects move on the
> screen. In order to make the objects move on the
> screen you had to specify the heading in degrees,
> like 90 degrees means East and 180 degrees means
> South. This was a first grade child; he didn't know
> about degrees, . . . but he had watched an older child
> doing this and he puzzled and he puzzled and he
> eventually figured out that it was a code; that num-
> bers are codes for directions and all he had to do was
> crack the code. The secret code is something very
> familiar to a six year old. The idea that angular mea-
> sure is like a code is a discovery about the nature of

a mathematical system. That's one example of what I call epistemology. (Tursman, 1982, p. 12)

Computers cannot serve as a substitute for children actively constructing knowledge. Children cannot learn mathematical concepts using calculators, nor can they learn them (construct them) from using programmed instruction programs on computers. But computers do hold considerable potential for engaging children in valid intellectual exercises. Programs such as Logo and procedures that encourage code breaking and "hacking" have value as constructive activities.

Not mentioned yet are the word-processing capabilities of computers. It seems probable that as microcomputers decrease in price, they will eventually replace typewriters because of their capabilities for editing and revising text, thereby eliminating the need for retyping. Familiarity with word processing is a *skill* that will certainly be worth developing.

Computers have a place in a Piagetian world. Computers are not sources of knowledge, but they are engaging machines that children can act on. Their greatest potential may not yet have been discovered. Lastly, Hofmann (1983) points out that judicious computer use in schools can have a positive effect on the *affective* life of the child.

Question 12: How does Piaget's theory differ from some of the other major theoretical positions in psychology?

Answer:[6] There are three major "streams" of psychological and educational thinking, each forming a theoretical position, each resting on a different set of assumptions (Langer 1969; Kohlberg and Mayer 1972). The assumptions of each theoretical position form the core around which each theory is constructed. Each evolves a different concept of the child. Each suggests different ways of "educating" the child. The three theoretical positions are referred to here as *romanticism-maturationism*, *cultural transmission-behaviorism*, and *progressivism-cognitive development* (Kohlberg and Mayer 1972).

Romanticism-Maturationism. Romanticism has its roots in the writings of Jean Jacques Rousseau. It is primarily a maturationist concept of development. Experience or the environment is important only insofar as it affects development by providing the necessary nourishment for the "naturally" growing organism. Genetically predetermined stages are seen as unfolding "naturally." Stages can be *fixated*, or arrested by experience, but the *course* of development is assumed to be innate, inborn, inherited, or genetically predetermined.

Maturationists such as Freud and Montessori hold that what comes from within the child is the most important aspect of development; therefore, the pedagogical (educational) environment should be permissive enough to allow the inner "good" (abilities and social virtues) to unfold and the inner "bad" to come under control (ibid., p. 451). Thus the child is conceptualized like a plant. It is begun from a seed, and all the characteristics that it can evolve and will evolve are predetermined and contained within the seed. The plant needs sunshine, air, and water (a good environment) in which to grow, but beyond retarding or maximizing growth, environmental factors do not have major effects on the characteristics of the plant.

Cultural Transmission-Behaviorism. The traditional education practiced in the United States and most Western societies is rooted in the concept that the job of education is the direct transmission of bodies of information, skills, and the values of the culture to the child. In the Soviet Union, this idea has been institutionalized as an explicit state policy.

The cultural transmission concept of development views the mind as a machine.[7] There are environmental "inputs" and behavioral "outputs," but the concept implies that the organism has little to do with its own development. The environment is assumed to be responsible for development. Underlying this mechanistic concept of development are such associationistic concepts as *stimulus and response* and *reinforcement*, which have their roots in the works of John Locke, Ivan Pavlov,

John Watson, A. H. Thorndike, and most recently, B. F. Skinner. Development of the child's mind, moral values, and emotions is seen as a result of specifically acquired associations under the control of the environment (via reinforcement).

Current educational innovations based on the cultural transmission rationale are *educational technology*[8] and *behavior modification*.[9] A clear application of these principles to preschool education can be found in the writings of Bereiter and Engleman (1966). In these views, external experience (or reinforcement) is considered critical in shaping or determining the course of learning and development. Maturation or genetic predeterminism is generally considered to be of little significance.

The cultural transmission-behaviorism model suggests that children can learn only through direct instruction. The teacher must teach the child. This is most efficiently carried out when the teacher (or parent) controls those reinforcers that work for a specific child and makes the receipt of reinforcement contingent on learning desired responses.

Progressivism-Cognitive Development. Underlying the progressive-cognitive development concept of learning and development is the amalgamation of the significance of both maturation and the environment (though the importance of the environment and maturation is construed entirely differently from their construction in the other two models). This is the interactionist viewpoint. Mental development is seen as the product of the interaction of the organism (the child) and the environment. This position was first elaborated by Plato, then early in this century by John Dewey, and most recently by Hans Werner and Jean Piaget.[10] The child is viewed neither as maturationally determined nor as a machine completely controlled by external agents. The child is a "scientist," an explorer, an inquirer; he or she is critically instrumental in constructing and organizing the world and his or her own development.[11]

NOTES

1. Roland Garcia is a physicist who worked with Piaget on a study of individual development and scientific development (Bringuier, 1980).

2. One of Piaget's major reservations about Freudian theory is the reliance on childhood memories for accurate information about the past.

3. Howard Gruber is professor of psychology and director of the Institute for Cognitive Studies at Rutgers University.

4. Research on computers and children is extremely limited. Some scholars feel that many claims made by Papert and other researchers are premature. An excellent review of research to date and also of important issues not yet resolved can be found in Pea and Kurland (1983).

5. Hacking "refers to a phenomenon which for lack of better terminology might be referred to as intellectual play with a microcomputer" (Hofmann 1983).

6. Adapted from Wadsworth 1978.

7. In my experience as a teacher in psychology and education I have found that many students reject the cultural transmission-behaviorism concept purely on emotional grounds. They are disturbed by the notion of considering themselves "machines" or even machinelike. Although the position of this book lies in large part in opposition to the behaviorist concept of development, one must be cautioned against rejecting things for purely emotional reasons. One is of course free to do so, and from certain perspectives, it is perfectly valid to do. But such a rejection is not based on the psychological truth or falseness of the question whether a human being is a "machine," a genetic map, or a unique organism playing a part in his or her own development.

8. "Educational technology" sounds like it means something more than it does. Basically, educational technology means the application of technological innovations to educational practice. This includes such things as computer-assisted instruction, teaching machines, programs, television, and other audiovisual devices. The assumptions underlying these techniques are generally the same as those of the cultural transmission concept of learning.

9. "Behavior modification" means the application of reinforcement techniques to educational or therapeutic practice. The term "behavior modification" is misleading because it refers to a specific technique among many techniques. Indeed, all people in

education, regardless of what techniques they are using, are involved in modifying behavior, whether they want to call it that or not.

10. Piaget was obviously not the only person working in developmental psychology in this area. Literally hundreds of others have made important contributions in recent years. Nevertheless, with the possible exception of Hans Werner, Piaget stood alone in the magnitude of his research over sixty years and in having generated a cohesive theory.

11. A caution was previously made regarding the rejection of psychological theories on emotional grounds. Similarly, one must caution against accepting psychological theories for emotional reasons. My experience has been that most people "like" Piagetian theory. They like the picture Piaget painted. Again, this is not evidence for the correctness or incorrectness of assertions nor adequate logical grounds for the acceptance of a theory. No doubt it is important for teachers to *like* and feel comfortable with whatever they use, however.

MISINTERPRETATIONS OF PIAGET'S THEORY

It is clear that the sixty years of research conducted by Jean Piaget on the development of knowledge in children has had a profound impact on psychological and educational theory. That we know more about how children develop mentally, how they learn, how they think, and how they reason because of Piaget's work is unquestionable. What is questionable is whether the rich knowledge Piaget left us will ever trickle down to the classroom teacher in a significant way and whether what trickles down will be distorted. Many "good ideas" have come down the road only to be popularized and distorted beyond recognition. It would be a great loss if the richness of Piaget's work is lost to education because of misinterpretation. Yet misinterpretations of myriad facets of Piaget's research are already commonplace. This section focuses on five common misconceptions about Piaget's work.

PIAGET DEVELOPED A THEORY OF EDUCATION

Piaget *did not* provide us with a theory of education or a curriculum for teaching. What he did offer is a research-backed conception of how children acquire and develop knowledge. Piaget's theory is not a recipe for better education. It is a body of knowledge and concepts that, to be of use to educators, must be integrated (assimilated and accommodated in Piaget's terms) into their existing knowledge.

The first step is to acquire a solid grasp of Piaget's theory of

---

Portions of the Appendix first appeared in "Misinterpretations of Piaget's Theory," *Impact on Instructional Improvement* 16, no.2 (1981): 1–11. Used by permission.

intellectual (cognitive, mental) development. For the beginner there are several excellent *introductory* works (Furth 1970; Ginsburg and Opper 1978; Phillips 1969; Pulaski 1971; Wadsworth 1979). Once you have a firm grasp on Piaget's theory (it will not come after one book), then you should be ready to begin to conceptualize teaching methods, curriculum, and children through the eyes of the theory.

Piaget's theory is a perspective from which you can evaluate the appropriateness and effectiveness of what you do as an educator, whether as a teacher or in curriculum or administration. When you begin to think about the application of Piagetian concepts to educational practice, there are several references that can be a source of ideas (see list of suggested readings at the back of this book).

CHILDREN ACHIEVE A STAGE OF DEVELOPMENT AT A CERTAIN AGE

The ages used by Piagetians to describe when particular mental characteristics occur are *average* ages. For example, the typical child develops, out of his or her *actions* on objects, the basic knowledge of number necessary to learn and comprehend simple addition around age 6. Some children develop this earlier—some at age 5, some at age 4—and a small percentage possibly earlier still. Some do not develop the same concept until age 7 or 8, or even later. Thus, within any set of children grouped according to chronological age there is a wide range of developmental differences with respect to the content they are capable of learning with comprehension. Children develop at different rates, and there are widely varying potentialities for learning in any group at any given point in time. Children with slower than average rates of development predictably do not master content as readily as other children do. They are frequently viewed as slow learners or as having learning problems. Indeed, to submit all children to the same curriculum with the same expectations is to invite, if not guarantee, failure and can be viewed as educational neglect.

THE TEACHER HAS NO ROLE

Some educators have concluded that because children develop knowledge out of their experiences in the environment, there is no place for the teacher in Piagetian theory. This is absolutely not true. What is true is that the teacher who is trying to teach in a manner consistent with Piaget's theory spends considerably less time lecturing at children and less time trying to get them to acquire knowledge through words and ditto sheets. But the role of the teacher is still central in a Piagetian classroom. The teacher is the one who largely decides the experiences of which the school environment will be composed. In addition, the teacher is in the best position to decide which children are ready for what experiences. There are several ways to get information about children's levels of cognitive development and what they are "ready" to learn. One is obviously to test them using Piagetian procedures. A second is through careful observation of children's reasoning in class. Another is to pay attention to children's "spontaneous interests." Intense interest is frequently a child's way of signaling us that he or she is "ready" (and highly motivated) to learn and discover particular things. A discussion of the value of spontaneous interests in intellectual development can be found in Wadsworth 1978.

BRAIN GROWTH CORRELATES
WITH PIAGETIAN STAGES

Work in neurosciences, called *brain growth periodization*, popularized primarily by Herman Epstein (1978, 1979) and Epstein and Teopfer (1978) has identified major growth periods, or "growth spurts," in the brain. These spurts are reported to correlate with Piaget's four main stages of intellectual development. Epstein has made a number of recommendations to educators, using the correlation between growth spurts and Piaget's main stages as support for his statements. His major contention seems to be that intellectual development proceeds *during* periods of brain growth but does not proceed *between* periods of brain growth. Implications are drawn from this conclusion.

Though Epstein's research is exciting in many respects, it seems inappropriate to draw support for Epstein's work from Piaget's work. There is nothing in Piaget's research that supports Epstein's views. Though Piagetians use the concept of stages to describe development, they also make clear that development is a continuum and not a series of discrete stages (Wadsworth 1979). Epstein's periods of brain growth can be viewed as discrete stages; Piaget's "stages" *cannot* be so viewed. Thus Epstein's correlation has no meaning.

In addition, Epstein writes: "... the brain growth hiatus between ages 12 and 14 years covers the junior high period, so we predict little increase in intellectual abilities during that period" (1979, p. 4). Again, there is nothing in Piagetian research that will support such an observation or prediction. Indeed, Piaget's research clearly indicates that intellectual development is more or less continuous over the age span.

While there are undoubtedly links between what goes on inside the brain and intellectual development, it does not yet seem clear what those links are or what educational conclusions can be reasonably drawn from them.

PIAGET HAS ALL THE ANSWERS

One of the greatest misinterpretations of Piagetian theory is that it has "all the answers." Nothing could be further from the truth. No theory has all the answers. Most theories have some utility for conceptualizing some educational issues and questions. It is an astute educator who can look at his or her educational practices from a variety of perspectives. Piagetian theory does offer an organized, coherent, empirically supported way to view the child and many educational practices.

Many of us who began our professional careers as public school teachers have been drawn to Piaget's work because it has provided validation for many of our intuitive but hard to justify beliefs about children and schools. Piaget's work has helped us to understand children and how they develop. Understanding children is the best way to improve teaching and curriculum. As David Elkind says:

> ... most of those who shape curricula, lack a developmental approach, ... they keep floundering around, looking for new approaches and new theories to give them relevance. They do not appreciate that knowing child development is the best way to develop curriculum materials." (Albin 1980, pp. 4–5)

Piaget provided us with a map of how children's minds develop. If we can master that map, we can eliminate some of the "floundering around."

BIBLIOGRAPHY

Alben, R. "David Elkind: Going Beyond Piaget." *APA Monitor* 11 (November 1980).

Bearison, D. "Role of Measurement Operations in the Acquisition of Conservation." *Developmental Psychology* 1 (1969): 653-60.

Bereiter C., and S. Engleman. *Teaching Disadvantaged Children in the Preschool.* Englewood Cliffs, N.J.: Prentice-Hall, 1966.

Bloom, B. *Stability and Change in Human Characteristics.* New York: John Wiley, 1964.

Bovet, M. "Piaget's Theory of Cognitive Development and Individual Differences." In *Piaget and His School,* edited by B. Inhelder and H. Chipman, pp. 269-79. New York: Springer-Verlag, 1976.

Brainerd, C. *Piaget's Theory of Intelligence.* Englewood Cliffs, N.J.: Prentice-Hall, 1978.

Bringuier, J. *Conversations with Jean Piaget.* Chicago: University of Chicago Press, 1980.

Carnegie Quarterly 23, no. 3 (Summer 1975).

Carroll, J., and J. Rest. "Moral Development." In *Handbook of Developmental Psychology,* edited by B. Wolman. Englewood Cliffs, N.J.: Prentice-Hall, 1982.

Copeland, R. *How Children Learn Mathematics.* 2d ed. New York: Macmillan, 1974.

Damon, W. "Conception of Positive Justice as Related to the Development of Logical Operations." *Child Development* 46 (1975): 301-12.

Dasen, P., ed. *Piagetian Psychology: Cross Cultural Contributions*. New York: Gardner Press, 1977.

Dewey, J. *Education and Experience*. New York: Colliers, 1963.

Duckworth, E. "The Having of Wonderful Ideas." *Harvard Educational Review* 42 (May 1972): 217-31.

———. "Either We're Too Early and They Can't Learn It, or We're Too Late and They Know It Already: The Dilemma of 'Applying Piaget.'" Pt. 2. *Genetic Epistemologist* 7, no. 4 (1978): 3-7.

Dupont, H. "Affective Development: Stage and Sequence (A Piagetian Interpretaion)." In *Adolescent Development in Education*, edited by R. Moser. Berkeley: McCutcheon (in press).

Easley, J. "Four Decades of Conservation Research." In *Knowledge and Development*. Vol 2, *Piaget and Education*, edited by J. Gallagher and J. Easley, pp. 139-76. New York: Plenum, 1978.

Elkind, D. "Children's Discovery of the Conservation of Mass, Weight, and Volume: Piaget's Replication Study II." *Journal of Genetic Psychology* 98 (1961a): 219-27.

———. "Quality Conceptions in Junior and Senior High School Students." *Child Development* 32 (1961b): 551-60.

———. "Quantity Conceptions in College Students." *Journal of Social Psychology* 57 (1962): 459-65.

———. "Egocentrism in Adolescence." *Child Development* 38 (1967): 1025-34.

———. "Cognitive Structures and Adolescent Experience." *Adolescence* 2 (1967-68): 427-34.

———. "Giant in the Nursery." *New York Times Magazine*, May 1968, p. 25.

———. "Piagetian and Psychometric Conceptions of Intelligence." *Harvard Educational Review* 39 (1969): 319-37.

———. *Child Development and Education: A Piagetian Perspective*. New York: Oxford University Press, 1976.

———. "Is Piaget Passe in Elementary Education?" *Genetic Epistemologist* 7, no. 4 (1978): 1-2.

Epstein, H. "Growth Spurts During Brain Development: Implications for Educational Policy and Practice." In *Education and the Brain*, edited by J. Chall and A. Mirsky, pp. 343-70. Chicago: University of Chicago Press, 1978.

———. "Brain Growth and Cognitive Functioning." *Colorado Journal of Educational Research* 19 (Fall 1979).

Epstein, J., and C. Teopfer. "A Neuroscience Basis for Reorganizing Middle School Education." *Educational Leadership* 35 (May 1978): 656-60.

Erickson, E. *Childhood and Society*. New York: Norton, 1950.

Evans, R. *Jean Piaget: The Man and His Ideas*. New York: Dutton, 1973.

Flavell, J. *The Developmental Psychology of Jean Piaget*. Princeton, N.J.: Van Nostrand, 1963.

————. "The Uses of Verbal Behavior in Assessing Children's Cognitive Abilities." In *Measurement and Piaget*, edited by P. Green, M. Ford, and G. Flamer, pp. 198-204. New York: McGraw-Hill, 1971.

Forman, G., and D. Kuschner. *The Child's Construction of Knowledge: Piaget for Teaching Children*. Belmont, Calif.: Brooks-Cole, 1977.

Freud, A. *The Ego and the Mechanisms of Defense*. New York: International Universities Press, 1946.

Furth, H. *Piaget for Teachers*. Englewood Cliffs, N.J.: Prentice-Hall, 1970.

Gallagher, J. "Reflexive Abstraction and Education: The Meaning of Activity in Piaget's Theory." In *Knowledge and Development*. Vol. 2, *Piaget and Education*, edited by J. Gallagher and J. Easley. New York: Plenum, 1978.

Gallagher, J., and D. Reid. *The Learning Theory of Piaget and Inhelder*. Monterey, Calif.: Brooks-Cole, 1981.

Gilligan, C. "In a Different Voice: Women's Conception of Self and of Morality." *Harvard Educational Review* 47 (1977): 481-517.

Ginsburg, H., and S. Opper. *Piaget's Theory of Intellectual Development*. 2d ed. Englewood Cliffs, N.J.: Prentice-Hall, 1978.

Goodnow, J., and G. Bethon. "Piaget's Tasks: The Effects of Schooling and Intelligence." *Child Development* 37 (1966): 573-82.

Greenfield, P. M. "On Culture and Conservation." In *Studies in Cognitive Growth*, edited by J. Bruner et al. New York: Wiley, 1966.

Gruber, H. *Darwin on Man: A Psychological Study of Scientific Creativity*. 2d ed. Chicago: University of Chicago Press, 1981.

Gruber, H., and J. Voneche, eds. *The Essential Piaget*. New York: Basic Books, 1977.

Gruen, G. E. "Experiences Affecting the Development of Number Conservation in Children." *Child Development* 36 (1965): 964-79.

Hall, G. *Adolescence*. 2 vols. New York: Appleton, 1908.

Heard, S., and B. Wadsworth. "The Relationship between Cognitive Development and Language Complexity." Manuscript, Mount Holyoke College, May 1977.

Hersh, R., D. Paolitto, and J. Reimer. *Promoting Moral Growth: From Piaget to Kohlberg.* New York: Longman, 1979.

Hofmann, R. "Would You Like a Bite of My Peanut Butter Sandwich?" *Journal of Learning Disabilities,* Spring 1983.

Hooper, I. H. "Piagetian Research and Education." In *Logical Thinking in Children,* edited by I. E. Sigel and F. H. Hooper, pp. 423-34. New York: Holt, Rinehart and Winston, 1968.

Hunt, J. McV. *Intelligence and Experience.* New York: Ronald Press, 1961.

Inhelder, B. "Outlook." In *Jean Piaget: Consensus and Controversy,* edited by S. Modgil and C. Modgil. New York: Holt, Rinehart and Winston, 1982.

———. *The Diagnosis of Reasoning in the Mentally Retarded.* New York: John Day, 1968.

Inhelder, B., and H. Chipman, eds. *Piaget and His School.* New York: Springer-Verlag, 1976.

Inhelder, B., and J. Piaget. *The Growth of Logical Thinking from Childhood to Adolescence.* Translated by Anne Parsons and Stanley Pilgram. New York: Basic Books, 1958.

———. *The Early Growth of Logic in the Child.* London: Routledge and Kegan Paul, 1964.

Kagan, J. "Emergent Themes in Human Development." *American Scientist* 64, no. 2 (March-April 1976): 186-96.

———. "Jean Piaget's Contributions." *Phi Delta Kappan,* December 1980, pp. 245-46.

Kamii, C. "Autonomy as the Aim of Education: Implications of Piaget's Theory." In Kamii, C., *Number in Preschool and Kindergarten,* Washington, D.C.: National Association for the Education of Young Children, 1982.

Kamii, C., and R. DeVries. *Physical Knowledge in Preschool Education: Implications of Piaget's Theory.* Englewood Cliffs, N.J.: Prentice-Hall, 1978.

Keegan, R. *The Evolving Self.* Cambridge, Mass.: Harvard University Press, 1982.

Kohlberg, L. "The Development of Modes of Moral Thinking and Choice in the Years Two to Sixteen." Ph.D. dissertation, University of Chicago, 1958.

———. "Early Education: A Cognitive-Developmental View." *Child Development* 39 (1968a): 1013-63.

———. "The Montessori Approach to Cultural Deprivation. A Cognitive Development Interpretation and Some Research Findings." In *Preschool Education, Theory, Research, and Action,* edited by R. Hess and R. Bear. Chicago: Aldine, 1968b.

——. "Stage and Sequence: The Cognitive-Developmental Approach to Socialization." In *Handbook of Socialization Theory and Research*, edited by D. Goslen, pp 347-408. Chicago: Rand McNally, 1969a.

——. *Stages in the Development of Moral Thought and Action*. New York: Holt Rinehart and Winston, 1969b.

——. "Moral Stages and Moralization: The Cognitive-Developmental Approach." In *Moral Development and Behavior: Theory, Research and Social Issues*, edited by T. Lickona. New York: Holt, Rinehart and Winston, 1976.

Kohlberg, L., and R. Mayer. "Development as the Aim of Education." *Harvard Educational Review* 42, no. 4 (November 1972): 449-96.

Kuhn, D.; N. Langer, L. Kohlberg, and N. Hann. "The Development of Formal Operations in Logical and Moral Judgment." *Genetics Psychology Monograph* 95 (1977): 115.

L'Abate, L. "Frequency of Citation Study in Child Psychology Literature." *Child Development* 40 (1968): 87-92.

Mermelstein, E., and L. Schulman. "Lack of Formal Schooling and the Acquisition of Conservation." *Child Development* 38 (1967): 39-52.

Neimark, E. "Adolescent Thought: Transition to Formal Operations." In *Handbook of Developmental Psychology*, edited by B. Wolman. Englewood Cliffs, N.J.: Prentice-Hall, 1982.

Overton, W., and J. Newman. "Cognitive Development: A Competence-Activation/Utilization Approach." In *Review of Human Development*, edited by T. Field et al. New York: Wiley, 1982.

Papert, S. *Mindstorms: Children, Computers and Powerful Ideas*. New York: Basic Books, 1980.

Pea, R., and D. Kurland. "On the Cognitive and Educational Benefits of Teaching Children Programming: A Critical Look." *New Ideas in Psychology* 1 (1983).

Phillips, J. *The Origins of Intellect: Piaget's Theory*. 2d ed. San Francisco: Freeman, 1969.

Piaget, J. *The Language and Thought of the Child*. New York: Harcourt Brace Jovanovich, 1926.

——. *Judgment and Reasoning of the Child*. New York: Harcourt Brace Jovanovich, 1928.

——. *The Child's Conception of Physical Causality*. New York: Harcourt Brace Jovanovich, 1930.

——. *The Child's Conception of Number*. London: Humanities Press, 1952a.

———. "Autobiography." In *History of Psychology in Autobiography*, edited by E. G. Boring et al., pp. 237-56. 4 vols. Worcester, Mass.: Clark University Press, 1952b.

———. *The Origins of Intelligence in Children*. New York: International Universities Press, 1952c.

———. *The Construction of Reality in the Child*. Translated by Margaret Cook. New York: Basic Books, 1954.

———. "The Genetic Approach to the Psychology of Thought." *Journal of Educational Psychology* 52 (1961): 275-81.

———. *Play, Dreams and Imitation in Childhood*. New York: Norton, 1962.

———. *The Child's Conception of the World*. Paterson, N.J.: Littlefield, Adams, 1963a.

———. *The Psychology of Intelligence*. Paterson, N.J.: Littlefield, Adams, 1963b.

———. "Three Lectures." In *Piaget Rediscovered*, edited by R. E. Ripple and U. N. Rockcastle. Ithaca, N.Y.: Cornell University Press, 1964.

———. *The Moral Judgment of the Child*. New York: Free Press, 1965.

———. *Six Psychological Studies*. New York: Vintage Books, 1967.

———. *The Mechanisms of Perception*. New York: Basic Books, 1969.

———. *Genetic Epistemology*. New York: Columbia University Press, 1970a.

———. *Science of Education and the Psychology of the Child*. New York: Viking Press, 1970b.

———. "The Theory of Stages in Cognitive Development." In *Measurement and Piaget*, edited by D. Green, M. Ford, and G. Glamer, pp. 1-7. New York: McGraw-Hill, 1971.

———. "Intellectual Evolution from Adolescence to Adulthood." *Human Development* 15 (1972): 1-12.

———. *The Principles of Genetic Epistemology*. New York: Basic Books, 1972b.

———. *To Understand Is to Invent*. New York: Viking Press, 1973.

———. "Need and Significance of Cross-Cultural Studies in Genetic Psychology." In *Cultures and Cognition: Readings in Cross Cultural Psychology*, edited by J. Berr and P. Dasen, pp. 299-309. London: Methuen, 1974a.

———. *Understanding Causality*. New York: Norton, 1974b.

———. "The Affective Unconscious and the Cognitive Unconscious." In *Piaget and His School*, edited by B. Inhelder and H. Chipman, pp. 63-71. New York: Springer-Verlag, 1976.

————. "Problems in Equilibration." In *Topics in Cognitive Development*. Vol. 1, *Equilibration: Theory, Research and Application*, edited by M. Appel and L. Goldberg, pp. 3-13. New York: Plenum, 1977a.

————. *The Development of Thought: Equilibrium of Cognitive Structures*. New York: Viking, 1977.

————. "Creativity." In *The Learning Theory of Piaget and Inhelder*, edited by J. Gallagher and K. Reid. Monterey, Calif.: Brooks-Cole, 1981b.

————. *Intelligence and Affectivity: Their Relationship During Child Development*. Palo Alto, Calif.: Annual Reviews, 1981a.

Piaget, J., and B. Inhelder. *The Child's Conception of Space*. London: Routledge and Kegan Paul, 1956.

————. *The Psychology of the Child*. Translated by Helen Weaver. New York: Basic Books, 1969.

Piaget, J., B. Inhelder, and A. Szeminska. *The Child's Conception of Geometry*. New York: Basic Books, 1960.

Pinard, A., and M. Laurendeau. "A Scale of Mental Development Based on the Theory of Piaget: Description of a Project." *Journal of Research in Science Teaching* 2 (1964): 253-60.

Pulaski, M. *Understanding Piaget*. New York: Harper Row, 1971.

Rosenthal, R., and L. Jacobson. *Pygmalion in the Classroom*. New York: Holt, Rinehart and Winston, 1968.

Schwebel, M., and J. Raph, eds. *Piaget in the Classroom*. New York: Basic Books, 1973.

Selman, R. L. "The Relation of Role-Taking to the Development of Moral Judgment in Children." *Child Development* 42 (1971): 59-91.

————. "Social-Cognitive Understanding: A Guide to Educational and Clinical Practice." In *Moral Development and Behavior: Theory, Research and Social Issues*, edited by T. Lickona. New York: Holt, Rinehart and Winston, 1976.

Sheehan, D., ed. *Piaget: Educational Perspectives*. Oneonta, N.Y.: State University College at Oneonta, 1979.

Sigel, I. E. "The Attainment of Concepts." In *Review of Child Development Research*. Vol. 1, edited by M. L. Hoffman and L. V. Hoffman, pp. 209-48. New York: Russell Sage Foundation, 1964.

Sigel, I. E., and F. H. Hooper. *Logical Thinking in Children: Research Based on Piaget's Theory*. New York: Holt, Rinehart and Winston, 1968.

Sinclair, H. "Piaget's Theory of Development: The Main Stages." In *Piagetian Cognitive-Development Research and Mathemat-*

ical Education, edited by M. Rosskopf, L. Steffe, and S. Taback. Washington, D.C.: National Council of Teachers of Mathematics, 1971.

Smedslund, J. "The Acquisition of Conservation of Substance and Weight in Children." In *Readings in Child Development and Behavior*, edited by G. Stendler. New York: Harcourt Brace Jovanovich, 1964.

Tursman, C. "Computers in Education." *School Administrator*, April 1982.

Uzgiris, I. "Situational Generality of Conservation." In *Logical Thinking in Children*, edited by I. E. Sigel and F. H. Hooper, pp. 40-52. New York: Holt, Rinehart and Winston, 1968.

Wadsworth, B. "The Effect of Peer Group Social Interaction on the Conservation of Number Learning in Kindergarten Children." Ed.D. dissertation, State University of New York at Albany, 1968.

———. *Piaget for the Classroom Teacher*. New York: Longman, 1978.

———. *Piaget's Theory of Cognitive Development*. 2d ed. New York: Longman, 1979.

———. "Piaget's Concept of Adaptation and Its Value to Educators." In *Piagetian Theory and the Helping Professions*. Eighth Annual Conference Proceedings. Los Angeles: University of Southern California (in press).

Wadsworth, B., and J. Cody. "Frequency of Citation in *Child Development* in 1974." Manuscript, Mount Holyoke College, n.d.

Wallach, L., J. Wall, and L. Anderson. "Number Conservation: The Roles of Reversibility, Addition, Subtraction, and Misleading Perceptual Cues." *Child Development* 38 (1967): 425-42.

Wohlwill, J., and R. Lowe. "Experimental Analysis of the Development of Conservation of Number." *Child Development* 33 (1962): 153-68.

Zimiles, H. "The Development of Differentiation and Conservation of Number." *Monograph Society for Research in Child Development* 31 (1966).

SUGGESTED READINGS

Piagetian Theory

Brainerd, C. *Piaget's Theory of Intelligence*, Englewood Cliffs, N.J.: Prentice-Hall, 1978.

Flavell, J. *The Developmental Psychology of Jean Piaget*. Princeton, N.J.: Van Nostrand, 1963.

Forman, G., and D. Kuschner. *The Child's Construction of Knowledge: Piaget for Teaching Children*. Belmont, Calif.: Brooks-Cole, 1977.

Furth, H. *Piaget and Knowledge: Theoretical Foundations*. Chicago: University of chicago Press, 1981.

Gallagher, J., and D. Reid. *The Learning Theory of Piaget and Inhelder*. Monterey, Calif.: Brooks-Cole, 1981.

Ginsburg, H., and S. Opper. *Piaget's Theory of Intellectual Development*. 2d ed. Englewood Cliffs, N.J.: Prentice-Hall, 1978.

Gruber, H., and J. Voneche, eds. *The Essential Piaget*. New York: Basic Books, 1977.

Piaget, J. *The Origins of Intelligence in Children*. New York: International Universities Press, 1952c.

——. *Six Psychological Studies*. New York: Vintage Books, 1967.

——. *Genetic Epistemology*. New York: Columbia University Press, 1970a.

——. *Science of Education and the Psychology of the Child*. New York: Viking Press, 1970b.

——. *To Understand Is to Invent*. New York: Viking Press, 1973.

——. *Intelligence and Affectivity: Their Relationship During Child Development*. Palo Alto, Calif.: Annual Reviews, 1981a.

Piaget, J., and B. Inhelder. *The Psychology of the Child*. Translated by Helen Weaver. New York: Basic Books, 1969.

Education

Elkind, D. *Child Development and Education: A Piagetian Perspective*. New York: Oxford University Press, 1976.

Forman, G., and F. Hill. *Constructive Play: Applying Piaget in the Preschool*. Monterey, Calif.: Brooks-Cole, 1980.

Furth, H. *Piaget for Teachers*. Englewood Cliffs, N.J.: Prentice-Hall, 1970.

Gallagher, J., and D. Reid. *The Learning Theory of Piaget and Inhelder*. Monterey, Calif.: Brooks-Cole, 1981.

Kamii, C. *Number in Preschool and Kindergarten*. Washington, D.C.: National Association for the Education of Young Children, 1982.

Kamii, C., and R. DeVries. *Physical Knowledge in Preschool Education: Implications of Piaget's Theory*. Englewood Cliffs, N.J.: Prentice-Hall, 1978.

Piaget, J. *Science of Education and the Psychology of the Child*. New York: Viking Press, 1970b.

Schwebel, M., and J. Raph, eds. *Piaget in the Classroom*. New York: Basic Books, 1973.

Sheehan, D., ed. *Piaget: Educational Perspectives*. Oneonta, N.Y.: State University College at Oneonta, 1979.

Wadsworth, B. *Piaget for the Classroom Teacher*. New York: Longman, 1978.

Arithmetic/Mathematics

Copeland, R. *How Children Learn Mathematics*. 2d ed. New York: Macmillan, 1974.

Ginsburg, H. *Children's Arithmetic: The Learning Process*. New York: Van Nostrand Co., 1977.

Kamii, C. *Number in Preschool and Kindergarten*. Washington, D.C.: National Association for the Education of Young Children, 1982.

Piaget, J. *The Child's Conception of Number*. London: Humanities Press, 1952a.

Piaget, J., B. Inhelder, and A. Szeminska. *The Child's Conception of Geometry*. New York: Basic Books, 1960.

Special Needs Education

Gallagher, J., and D. Reid. *The Learning Theory of Piaget and Inhelder*. Monterey, Calif.: Brooks-Cole, 1981.

Inhelder, B. *The Diagnosis of Reasoning in the Mentally Retarded*. New York: John Day, 1968.

Inhelder, B., and H. Chipman, eds. *Piaget and His School*. New York: Springer-Verlag, 1976.

Wadsworth, B. *Piaget for the Classroom Teacher*. New York: Longman, 1978.

Moral Reasoning

Cowan, P. *Piaget with Feeling*. New York: Holt, Rinehart and Winston, 1978.

Gilligan, C. "In a Different Voice: Women's Conception of Self and of Morality," *Harvard Educational Review* 47 (1977): 481-517.

Hersh, R., D. Paolitto, and J. Reimer. *Promoting Moral Growth: From Piaget to Kohlberg*. New York: Longman, 1979.

Kohlberg, L. *The Philosophy of Moral Development: Moral Stages and the Idea of Justice*. San Francisco: Harper and Row, 1981.

Lickona, T., ed. *Moral Development and Behavior: Theory, Research and Social Issues*. New York: Holt, Rinehart and Winston, 1976.

Piaget, J. *The Moral Judgment of the Child*. New York: Free Press, 1965.

———. *Six Psychological Studies*. New York: Vintage Books, 1967.

———. *Intelligence and Affectivity: Their Relationship During Child Development*. Palo Alto, Calif.: Annual Reviews, 1981a.

INDEX

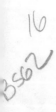